The Greening of Mrs. Duckworth is a refreshing and easily
read portrayal of spiritual growth. It takes a young girl—
overly protected, lonely, rejected and easily hurt—through
the joys of marriage, children, and hard work, to the secure
knowledge that she is not alone, that God cares. It pictures the
struggle to accept the fact that God understands her failures
and still loves her.

For anyone in the midst of such a search, this book will
lead the way to a real, spiritual experience. And the writing
is fascinating.

RUTH STAFFORD PEALE

Not only is this a lovely tale of the becoming of one woman, it is
a tale beautifully told. Mrs. Duckworth's gift of expression,
her fresh word choices, her unique life views, her power to
evoke mood and time and place, are a delight to read.

KAREN BURTON MAINS

The Greening of Mrs. Duckworth

by *Marion Duckworth*

Tyndale House
Publishers, Inc.
Wheaton, Illinois

Back cover photo by Mark
Duckworth.

All Scripture quotations are
from the Berkeley Version.

Library of Congress Catalog
Card Number 79-67857
ISBN 0-8423-1187-4, paper
Copyright © 1980 by
Marion Duckworth.
All rights reserved.
Second printing, October 1980.
Printed in the United States
of America.

CONTENTS

1

Tomorrow, Lord,
tomorrow,
I'll remove my mask
and people will have
to stop
and notice me . . .
Tomorrow, when I'm
older and stronger
Because today
I'm too alone.

Excerpt from "Tomorrow, But Not Today"
from Norman C. Habel, *Interrobang*
(Philadelphia: Fortress Press, 1969), pp. 26, 27.
© 1969 by Fortress Press. Reprinted with
the permission of the publishers.

One/ UNMASKED

Rage that had been stored in tightly sealed inner compartments finally burst its doors. As I hurled a pair of discarded pajamas against the wall, words tore from my throat and slashed the parsonage silence.

"God help me," I screamed. "I don't know who I am!"

Tears streaked my face and melted the layers of "peace and joy" that had been carefully applied like thick stage makeup. The "biblically correct" minister's wife's costume of smiles and understanding nods, a costume I'd worn for ten years, fell to the floor. Without it, I was as naked as though my clothes had been ripped off at high noon on Main Street.

That morning, I had stood at the stove: two eggs over medium; two eggs scrambled easy; two eggs with no icky white showing. Before-school prayers; the bus scurry. A husbandly kiss and, "See you at noon but don't worry if I'm late—goodbye."

Nothing unusual. Same alarm clock. Same faded bathrobe. Same sounds: whistling in the shower, water running in the bathroom basin. Radio. Coffee pot plop-plop, plop-plop. The sounds gradually trailed off until there was only the last door slam and the roar of the car as it pulled out of the driveway.

I moved into the kitchen and began to wipe early morning from the table and stove top. My hands, prisoners of my brain, trembled out distress signals, and the mayonnaise jar clattered against the butter dish as I put it back in the refrigerator.

Nearly a year before, my husband Jack, our three sons, and I had driven across the bridge to this island for the first time.

"There it is," Jack had said as he pulled up in front of the parsonage, a white split-level house that reigned on a shore-lined hillside, wearing terraced lawns and rock gardens like a jewel-bedecked green velvet robe.

"Wow!" one of our sons exploded. "Are you sure this is the right place?"

Members of our new congregation greeted us on the deck and took us on a tour of the house while we waited for the moving van to arrive.

Since Jack had become a rural pastor, we'd lived in tiny houses that bristled with resentment because we had too many children and too much furniture, and aged houses that moaned as they gasped for breath, burdened with layers of paint and wallpaper and pain in their creaking rheumatic boards. There had never been one like this.

We stood in the living room on wall-to-wall carpeting in front of a glass-enclosed fireplace and stared out the picture window at the driftwood-lined beach below. "Beach access right down the hill," one of the group told us. We moved into the kitchen. "Plenty of storage space," she went on, opening cabinets that revealed shelves already lined with cans, boxes, and packages of food put there by members of the congregation.

We went downstairs and looked at a bedroom and adjoining bath. "We thought that perhaps your sons could play here on rainy days," one of the women told us as she showed us an enclosed basement area.

That summer, as we sat down to lunch on the deck while hummingbirds hovered at the feeder, we prayed: "Thank you, Lord, for this food and this place." We prayed it again as we grilled hot dogs on the beach, our pockets full of sea urchins and sand dollars and our bodies tired from playing ball in the sand with our sons. "Thank you, God, for this place," we whispered at evening prayers, remembering Sunday services in the Community Church on the other side of the island when, with the sun shining through the cross set in stained glass behind Jack's pulpit, someone had bowed his heart in submission to Jesus Christ.

Now, I stood in *House and Garden* parsonage on postcard island crashing glasses and frying pans indiscriminately into the sink and watching chunks of minister's wife composure crack and fall around me. Occupants of the houses around ours had left for city apartments and condominiums; post-summer silence had settled like a cover over their driveways and shore-lined homes. I was alone.

Other mornings, I'd kept busy performing my homemaker, wife, mother, and minister's wife roles. Jobs to be done. A race to run. A God to please.

Scrub grease from stove top. Scrape dirt from cracks on counter top. Minister's wife has clean kitchen. Sort clothes in hamper. Minister's wife's clothes hamper never bulges with too many dirty clothes. Wash clothes. Fold properly. Dust window sill. Spot on rug. Shampoo and brush. Scrub. Still there. Scrub again. Keep scrubbing parsonage rug. Minister's house very clean.

Other days I'd been able to hide behind a Sunday best, three-for-a-quarter stickum smile and a wide-eyed stare.

Other days. But not today.

Today, I stood sobbing in my house-on-the-hill with gleaming stainless steel sinks and stove with a hood and exhaust fan on a tile floor with no wax buildup from

decades of tenants. I had gifts of fresh crab in the
refrigerator and a quarter of beef in the freezer. I bent
and picked up pieces of smile and splintered fragments
of pseudo-me and tried to fit them back together.

Hopeless.

I ran from the kitchen down the stairs, retracing every
morning's trail to unmade beds, still seeking rumpled
covers and dirty clothes to hide behind. Between the twin
beds, the person I'd long pretended to be suddenly
shattered completely, scattering professional piety over the
carefully vacuumed parsonage rug, and exposing a self
long hidden.

That self screamed, shuddering at the sound of its
own words:

"God help me; I don't know who I am!"

The island was listening intently to its own sounds:
a fisherman to the slap-slap of water against his boat; a
housewife to the hum of her washing machine. Mechanics
listened for motors that were missing. None heard the
pastor's wife screaming in the parsonage. But God, who'd
been listening for a single sparrow to fall, heard.

God heard.

Two/ REJECTED

In the beginning there is Mother's hand. She warms the
milk and takes on the world, softening its blows and
censoring its evil. Life goes on inside a warm cocoon. But
Mother cannot always tame the lions.

At the first sign of spring, Mother and I put on old
sweaters and made our way through rows of grape arbors
to the path at the edge of the woods that backed our
farmhouse. Starting at the humpy-backed camel tree, we
walked holding hands, my child's hand covered by hers,
until the pathway narrowed and we had to walk single file.

As far as we could tell, we were alone. On days like
this, the woods' mystery was buds and blossoms, new
shoots and scurrying creatures.

Trails embroidered our woods, and Mother knew each
one's destination. She chose; I followed. Some led to
clusters of may pinks growing delicately beneath piles of
dry leaves. Other paths led to slender lady slippers that
grew singly and serenely at the foot of a protective tree.
Still another led to an old car body that some unknown
vagrant (whose mysterious daytime invisibility fascinated
me) had made his nighttime home.

It never occurred to me to be afraid. Mother was there

and had walked the trails when she was a little girl like me. With a magic that mystified me, she could direct me to an ordinary-looking crust of brown leaves and stand waiting while I brushed them aside to uncover our first patch of may pinks. The moment we caught a glimpse of color, we'd look at each other and smile.

With Mother at my side, the woods was like a full-color illustration in my fairy tale book. It was life as life should always be—bright with daytime and filled with happy endings. Someone was there to take care of me, to make me feel protected and loved.

Mother had always been there, rising early to warm the kitchen, start the oatmeal, and lay out boots and mittens against the snow, creating a regulated environment. We were two alone in house, apartment, and springtime woods.

Mother guarded the doors and windows. We sat squeezed close in the big chair and listened to Lux Radio Theater. From her, I learned to measure sugar and cocoa, stir the fudge, peek and test as it cooled and hardened on the window ledge, and finally cut it into squares, lifting out two pieces with the tip of the knife blade.

Grade school years were a mother protectorate. "Come home right after school. Don't play with Sylvia—she has bugs in her hair. Eat all your lunch. Wear a sweater today. I'll be there right after school to take you across the big street."

Her love fashioned a springtime childhood—one pictured in our woods visits—doll carriage years spent encircled by Mother's arms in a world as peaceful as the eye of a storm. Her arms held me; her words loved me. I knew that I belonged. A flesh-of-my-flesh relationship, pressed into my memory like the flowers we picked, folded between pieces of waxed paper, and put between pages of the Bible. Years later, they still retained their delicate texture and beauty, as did the days of sunlight, security, and peace.

Notwithstanding poverty. Potatoes and beans,

potatoes and tomatoes, potatoes and eggs, potatoes and peas. Spaghetti and catsup. Spam stew: cube one can Spam, simmer in tomato sauce with two carrots, two large potatoes, one onion. Makes two dinners for two.

Notwithstanding slum apartments, relief, food coupons (fifty cents a day for food and one dollar a month for ice), WPA workroom clothing.

Notwithstanding Daddy in the asylum. Daddy, who could speak seven languages, who knew why birds could fly and how tall the pyramids are. Daddy, a son of Abraham, Jew of New York City by way of Romania. Address in care of State Hospital. Diagnosis: schizophrenic catatonic. Prognosis: incurable.

Notwithstanding Jewish persecution.

"Name Marion Siegel? Jew, ain't you?"

"No. My father is a Jew, my mother is a Christian. I'm being raised according to her religion."

"Yeah, yeah, sure."

Notwithstanding. Not as long as Mother could wall up my world with herself. With sweat, sleepless nights, and prayers that couldn't be uttered, she determinedly formed a childhood like a walk in the springtime woods.

But Mother couldn't always act as maternal sentinel. She had to let me go alone and watch from the window until I disappeared, as she did on the afternoons when I ran through the woods to get to my best friend Alice's house. On those trips I saw no buds, blossoms, or green shoots. Every scurrying creature became an enemy.

For hours, Alice and I laid out our paper dolls on her sunporch floor. My Mary Anne doll and her Brenda doll went swimming together, met handsome boyfriends, and rushed on paper legs from date to date. As soon as the street lights came on (the signal to go home), we put away our paper dolls.

Alice and I walked to the edge of the clearing. There she waited while I ran down the path through the woods. The tall trees clustered together into a black circle ready to suck me in, and I dared not stop to tie a shoelace. Finally,

I reached the other side, stepped into the clearing, and yelled, "OK!" Alice answered, "OK!" and I was safe again.

Going to Alice's house through the woods became a gray memory, like the time I had whooping cough all summer. In those woods at dusk, I was never tempted to stop and play, to search for berries, or to examine a flower, for I was alone. Alone, afraid, helpless . . . .

Gray shadows lengthened on my life. I added inches, developed a bust, and walked high school corridors past girls in color-coordinated sweaters and skirts, each coupled with a boy. Boys pinned their girls to the corridor wall with one arm and slid pencils down their sweaters. At 3:15 P.M., they walked down the steps and along the sidewalk together (the girls scuffing their loafers on the cement), slipped around the corner, cut across the street, and disappeared into middle class security.

Poverty mattered now. Daddy in the asylum mattered now. Jewishness mattered now. Rejection was an ugly rawboned intruder who elbowed her way into my teens demanding the front row of my life. She worked persistently until she achieved. Year after year I sat where she taught me that I belonged, in the far corners of classrooms where I reached out occasionally to others whom she had pushed into corners of fear. Mother stood helplessly at the edge of teenage, a housedressed figure waiting with after-school bread and jelly.

The door of the classroom was open that afternoon, and I could see girls lounging against the wall and sitting on desks, their sweater sleeves pushed up to their elbows, the folds of their skirts carefully draped.

"You're not going to tell Marion about the party, are you?"

"You know how it is. I already told you. My mother won't let me go unless Marion goes. You don't think I like it, do you?"

"For crying out loud. You'd think she was your sister or something. It's always that way."

"Well, she knows that we don't want her. I told her so myself."

I walked to them; the girls turned and stared. Then several of them laughed—a series of high-pitched bubbles that floated out of the open windows, down the streets, and into ears that knew exactly what the sounds meant.

Saturday night. Date night. Movies, dances at the community hall, parties in someone's rec room. I stood before the bedroom mirror fluffing my hair, adjusting a ruffle, turning, swirling, and turning again.

Eight o'clock. He said eight o'clock. The alarm clock on an embroidered dresser doily showed that it was time. Downstairs in the tavern below our second floor apartment, the juke box blasted "Don't Fence Me In," launching Saturday night. Customers' beer-bathed laughter rose between songs.

Eight-thirty. "Are you sure he said eight o'clock?"

"Yes, Mother. I'm sure."

She opened a magazine and held it like a shield in front of her, her jaw set hard.

Nine o'clock. I told him where I live. Didn't he understand? "Second floor over the downtown tavern— you know, it's on Front Street."

"Sure, I know. I can find it all right."

Nine-thirty. Downstairs they ordered another round. Laughter knifed from their world to mine and carved SATURDAY NIGHT across my chest. Dorsey's Boogie. Door slam. "Hey, how ya doin'?" Yell, scream, yahoo . . . . Saturday night sound effects trespassing upon my sorrow.

I pulled the cretonne curtain aside and looked out at the town, its weekday life gone with the pulling of plugs and the locking of doors. Mr. Leon, the dry goods merchant, had straightened his fabric bolts and driven home to Mrs. Leon. Harry had taken in his "Today's Special" sign from the sidewalk in front of the luncheonette. The Greek had secured strawberry and chocolate for the weekend and chased the cat out of the

front window of the ice cream parlor. He turned out the
lights except for one over the register, rang "no sale," and
stood in the dimness, counting. The bank had locked up
the town's money and the shoe repair man had lined up
the town's shoes ready to resole and reheel on Monday
morning when owners and managers and salesclerks would
bring weekday life, business-as-usual, to the buildings
again.

I left the window and walked through our railroad-
style apartment, through the kitchen, passing Mother who
sat at the kitchen table drinking tea and staring at the hot
water heater, to my bedroom. There in front of the mirror,
I shed hope with each piece of clothing and let it fall in a
pile at my feet.

Downstairs, the Saturday night finale. Their vowels
and consonants slurred, they joined in Budweiser
fellowship: "Gee, it's great to see that ole gang of
mine . . . " As I turned out the light I saw that the clock
on the dresser had pushed Saturday night into yesterday.

On Monday morning, I conjugated French verbs,
heavy with Saturday night's shame, and crept through
the day with obscurity pulled around me like a cloak.
Eventually, I had to face him.

"Sorry about Saturday," he said.

Silence.

"You see, I . . . I mean . . . I didn't know."

Silence.

"I mean, I didn't know you were a Jew. I have my
reputation. Know what I mean?"

Back home, I dropped my books on the table in the
living room next to the big chair in which Mother and I
used to sit together and listen to Lux Radio Theater. We
couldn't sit together anymore; years had come between us.

I was branded a Jew among Gentiles . . . a girl who
lived on county welfare . . . the daughter of an insane
man.

I hated myself.

Three/ MATES

Mother lived only twenty-four hours after the car in which
she was a passenger smashed into a truck. I telephoned a
second-hand furniture dealer to come and strip our
railroad flat bare. He arranged our tables, beds, and
dressers in his store alongside Mrs. Anderson's plush sofa
and Mrs. Brown's washstand and labeled them $5.75,
$12.50, and $4.00.

Nearly three years before, I'd walked across the high
school auditorium stage and received my diploma. Then I
had been hired by a short-wave radio receiving station to
send morse code and teletype messages to New York City
for eight hours a day. No more first-of-the-month relief
checks. Now I had a checking account, money for ham and
roast beef, yards of brown and blue from Mr. Wagner's
bolts, and hot fudge sundaes at the Greek's.

Sunday evenings, Mother and I had gone to the
movie house around the corner. We watched Richard
Conte get his man, as we ate chocolate bars brought from
home and washed them down with soda pop from the
lobby.

But now Mother was dead, her fierce, maternal eye
closed. I moved into a boarding house among friendly

strangers: breakfast at seven and dinner at six, clean sheets and towels once a week, and parlor privileges.

Love came. We became engaged and I moved again, this time to New York City so that I could be near him.

Evenings when I was with Jack, I was the guest of honor at a gigantic party the city was staging for me. Without him, the city seemed to be a stone giant that pleased and frightened me. Its streets led from apartment to office to dinner to shops to apartment. Its sounds rose from the pavement and seeped through cracks in the buildings.

It offered populated anonymity. No street-corner knots of boys and girls, fellow alumni of English 4, purring at one another through faint smiles, before whom I had to pass on my way to the Greek's. No need to pretend elaborate preoccupation with the cracks in the sidewalk because I dared not risk a single "Hello."

In New York City, there was everybody. Men in Hart, Schaffner, and Marx suits moved from cab to awning-covered restaurant. Lacquered girls picked their way through cafeteria lines while men in sagging trousers and long overcoats tried not to be noticed as they made lunch out of a cup of hot water and catsup in the automat.

I was glad to be a stranger among strangers, yet as I stood in front of Macy's department store and watched the 5:00 P.M. commuters sweep around me and pour into the subway tunnel, the crowdedness of the city seemed to threaten my significance. They pushed their way to the doors of their furnished rooms, apartments, or houses in the suburbs, where they would read the *Daily News* or the *New York Times*. Separate someones, allergic to chocolate or crazy about peanuts. Without Jack, I was just one more someone.

His love gave me significance. He was gentle and kind and tucked my hand under his arm as we crossed city streets. We walked Rockefeller Plaza's underground maze, stopping to look in windows at displays of silver, jade, and

handwoven cloth from India. In a jewelry shop, he bought
me a tiny blue locket and fastened it around my neck.
Upstairs on the street level, we bought ice cream cones
and sat close together on a bench near the huge fountain,
watching people pass. Across the fountain, tourists sat
under colored umbrellas at outdoor tables ordering roast
beef from long menus.

Flags from every nation perched on poles surrounding
the Center. Each was a country standing tall and silent
next to its neighbor, making this place a whole world. In
precious plots of earth tulips bloomed, celebrating our
love. We stooped to examine their petals, not noticing the
gum wrappers and cigarette butts that littered the
sidewalks.

On Sixth Avenue, we strolled together savoring the
mystery of each new shop, each restaurant. Tiny figures
carved from ivory, ancient polished gold coins lying in
plush boxes, a single Steuben glass bowl displayed on
midnight velvet—these were our wildflowers, our meadow.
The city's wide avenues and narrow side streets, its smug
skyscrapers and modest brownstones were our rocks to
climb on, our caves to explore. Manhattan was our own
island, a place of endless adventure. We sat on the grass
at Central Park, we ate bagels and drank cream soda in
delicatessen restaurants. Downtown, we peered into
Chinatown's grocery stores.

On a cold Sunday in December, Jack and I set off
down a street like children on our way to a party, moving
quickly through the sharp winter air, lone explorers on a
mission. We were seeking a church in which to be
married.

*Today we will choose a church, make an appointment
with the minister for the second day of January, and fresh
into the New Year, we will be married.*

We'd touched hearts at Radio City Music Hall while
we watched the Rockettes' famed high-kicking synchronized
chorus line, and at a midtown theater while Judy Holliday

sulked and Paul Douglas roared on stage in *Born
Yesterday*. Alone in Jack's parents' apartment and backed
by the sounds of buses roaring uptown beneath our
windows, we agreed to share a lifetime.

"I want to be married in a church," I'd insisted. He
had smiled patronizingly, having long ago left churches
behind. "If it will make you happy," he said. We made
a solemn agreement to choose a church by walking south
and stopping at the first one that was of a familiar
denomination.

That afternoon, garment workers sat by the windows
of their apartments reading the *Daily News;* clusters of
secretaries and file clerks and their boyfriends lunched in
the east side restaurants that we passed. With our warmest
jackets buttoned high and scarves tucked tightly around
our necks, we walked through the Sunday city. Our ears
began to redden with cold. I put one hand deep into the
pocket of his jacket and we moved in rhythm for several
blocks until we came to a church. Gray stone. A familiar
name. It was The One.

On January second at 8:00 P.M. flanked by our best
man and maid of honor, we stood before the minister in
his study and listened while he repeated carefully cut out
words that united us before God. In that tiny corner of the
great stone church on a block where buildings melted into
other buildings, we smiled and received congratulations
and best wishes. Had we been standing before a polished
desk surrounded by walls lined with theology books and
hung with framed diplomas—a room without flowers or
burning candles? It had not seemed so at all. Later, we
ate from the same slice of wedding cake and whispered my
new name to one another.

Across the street in a basement Italian restaurant that
we'd chosen as our own, we were served chicken cacciatore
by Maurice, a waiter who might have served pheasant to a
king. He'd watched our love grow across minestrone soup
and eggplant parmesan, standing guard over us at a

discreet distance while we ate each meal. Tonight, our
wedding night, he served the meal superbly, making sure
that the cloth was sparkling white, the silver gleaming,
and the food perfect.

Suitcases packed, we took the Hudson Tubes to
Newark, New Jersey, to spend our weekend honeymoon.
Subway cars were our golden chariots and conductors our
footmen. Next morning, we watched while a chef wearing
a tall white hat baked our butter cakes and scrambled our
eggs on a window grill in Child's Restaurant.

Back in New York at our jobs, we nestled like mated
birds among millions of New Yorkers. We did our special
things: ate corned beef sandwiches in a midtown
delicatessen, walked across Manhattan's 57th Street,
stopping to study paintings in small gallery windows.
We floated like kites through cool evenings. Spaghetti
on Third Avenue; the twenty-five cent cantaloupe and
ice cream special at Walgreen's fountain.

We were lovers alone on a park bench. Men in
business suits and women in black dresses and high heeled
patent leather shoes walked past us. Minutes ticked by,
measured on a clock, one single watchful eye set in the
tower of a tall insurance company building. Children
sprayed each other from a little drinking fountain. The
fountain, the clock, our certain bench, developed identities
of their own, populating our world.

I loved. I was loved. Two-become-one filled the
empty spaces. Jack's arms, his words, reassured me that he
loved me. They soothed the cowering teenager within. I
gorged myself with his love, his acceptance. But no matter
how much he gave, it was never enough.

Four/ GOD?

Saturday. No Monday to Friday quick orange drink, donut, and coffee at Nedick's eaten standing up. No 8:00 A.M. bus to the office.

Instead, we slept until we woke up. Stretched our toes to the end of the bed. Measured hands. Wrote words on one another's back: "I L-O-V-E Y-O-U."

"Two whole days together," we marveled. "Mr. and Mrs. and two whole days."

Joined in love and licensed by the State of New York. A new page in the family Bible: "Marion Siegel wed John Duckworth January 2, 1948." Us. Ours.

We'd come to each other by way of Boy Scout merit badges and Miss McCutcheon in the first grade; by way of pheasant hunting with Grandpa and hopscotch on the sidewalk. From John Duckworth, Nutley, New Jersey, and Marion Siegel, Bronx, New York, to Mr. and Mrs. John Duckworth of Manhattan. From bedrooms with Ingrid Bergman photos on the wall to two rooms, kitchenette, and bath. Incinerator down the hall. We'd grabbed a few decades from history and were holding them hopefully in our hands.

For $110 a month, we'd purchased construction

company privacy, a unit identical to all other units, one of many cubicles set side by side and stacked high. Last tenant's nail holes had been filled in; his marks had been painted over, his sounds had faded, his leavings incinerated. The rooms sat naked and waiting for our bed and sofa (here against the wall or over there under the window?), our one dollar art prints to be hung on its walls, and our name to be printed on the mailbox in the lobby.

Saturday morning ritual: clean and polish. We worked as carefully as any top level scientist in his laboratory, setting the front and sides of our world in order, and calling to one another every few minutes from the bedroom, the kitchen. He vacuumed, I scrubbed the tub. He emptied the garbage, I polished the glass-topped coffee table that had been a wedding present. He wiped city soot from the windowsills, I changed the sheets. Together we cleaned out the refrigerator.

Our clothes hung side by side in the closet; our shoes lined expectantly on the floor. His razor and my curlers, his after shave and my perfume together on the bathroom shelf.

Marion Siegel of the welfare Siegels, descended from schizophrenia and Jewishness, had become Duckworth. Duckworth née Siegel. Born Siegel become Duckworth.

The venetian blinds that fenced out Lexington Avenue, the gray sofa, the chair, the hammered aluminum tray from a best friend were symbols of my new identity. I caressed them as I worked. I loved the dime store glasses decorated with green and black flowers, the tiny casserole dishes (perfect for two), the dish towels embroidered by Jack's mother in red and yellow: "Monday, wash day; Tuesday, ironing," and the set of measuring cups nested in the drawer next to the wooden spoons and pancake turner. I loved to take these things in my hands. They assured me that I was someone important.

Jack and I took the laundry down to the basement in

the elevator and loaded it into machines. While our towels
and sheets swished in suds, 2G told us about the noisy
couple in 3G. We talked about the scarcity of city
apartments. We tutted and tsked and were cautiously
friendly. Then, our laundry dry and folded, 2G smiled a
vague, city-neighbor smile. "See you down here again. Or
maybe in the elevator."

Work over; time to play. We locked the apartment,
rode the elevator to the street, and waited on the corner
for a bus to take us uptown.

Fifth Avenue streets were carefully manicured; store
windows dressed and polished and ready for us. Displays
were full of our future: sleek, simple Swedish modern
furniture, a thick pile carpet. Colorful kitchen gadgets
lined the windows of Woolworth's where we each bought a
frozen malted milk, "the drink you eat with a spoon," for
ten cents, an investment we could afford. For twenty cents,
we bought a memory.

We walked hand in hand and talked. I began:
"When I was a little girl, I had a doll that drank from a
bottle and wet its diapers. Once, I took it on a visit to my
aunt's house and showed her how it worked. We didn't
have carpets on our floors at home; her carpets were thick,
wall-to-wall. I was so proud of my new doll that I stood
right there in the middle of her carpeted living room and
fed my doll a bottle. Then we all watched her make a
puddle on the floor."

Block after block, we recreated memories.

"Know how I got this scar over my eye?" Jack asked.
"I was on a Boy Scout camp-out, chopping wood for a
fire. Using all my muscles, I swung the ax and, *zowie,* a
piece flew up and hit me right here." We stopped, and
I touched the scar gently, reaching back with him through
the years.

We walked, swinging arms. We paused to watch a
Slinky spring toy bounce back and forth in one drugstore
window, and a long-necked wooden bird dip and bob into

a half-empty glass of water in another. We talked about Ginny from the office and Carl who lived upstairs. We planned a trip to Hawaii or Paris and an A-frame on the shore. Together, we approved a black evening gown and vetoed a frumpish-looking suit.

"When I was in high school," I told Jack, "I had an imitation leopard coat with red trim and lining. I wore it to Sunday school and felt like a movie star." I went on to review the pranks we played on our teacher. "One morning, we sneaked into the room early and removed all the chairs."

Jack drew his next words out slowly. "You've been in Sunday school and church most of your life, right?"

"Right."

"Well, I haven't. Tell me—what do you know about God? Tell me about him."

Tell you about God? Who, me?

Invisible, protective quills bristled all over me. Although I'd spent years in Sunday school memorizing the Ten Commandments, the Lord's Prayer, and the Twenty-third Psalm (until I could say the Psalm taking only two breaths), I knew almost nothing about God. Why hadn't I been introduced to him on one of those Sunday mornings when Mother and I paid our weekly respects to him, dressing carefully before we left home as though he would inspect us for torn hems or missing buttons?

Jack was waiting for an answer. "What can you tell me about God?" he persisted.

"I believe in him," I began. "I know that he exists . . . ."

"Suppose, for the sake of our conversation, I give you that," he countered. "What difference would that fact make to me?"

I reached back through the years, picking through old Sunday school lessons frantically. How could I have spent so many years in church and know so little about God?

Jack went on: "What about Jesus Christ? Who is he?"

"Jesus Christ is—well—he's like God, but less than God," I began feebly.

"Is he just a man or what?"

His questions glared at me, demanding answers. God was an idea that I wanted to be true. He had been my secret savings account, my egg money in the cookie jar....

We'd been standing on the corner waiting for the bus to take us back to our apartment. It came; crowds pushed around us. Jack steered me up the steps, fished in his pocket for change, and maneuvered us to the back of the bus and into an empty seat. We left the Swedish modern furniture and thick pile carpets in their window displays. But our unfinished conversation crowded between us like an unwelcome seat companion.

Church was as foreign to our city life as cows and the Eiffel Tower. Uptown churches seemed forbidding. Some wore their angled roofs like tipped berets and smirked at us when we passed. Others, like one tucked discreetly between apartment buildings—homes of corporation presidents, their wives, children, and maids—seemed to warn: *by invitation only.* A few blocks from our apartment was an aged brick church, one we'd passed many times. It looked as old as the city itself. Yet it didn't droop with chipped bricks or dirtied windows, but had grown old quietly, like a dignified great-grandmother.

I missed Sunday morning in a familiar sanctuary, missed singing hymns and contemplating God—missed feeling safely sanctioned by him. One Sunday morning, after scrambled eggs at our formica-topped dinette table, we wiped crumbs, folded the *Daily News* neatly on the coffee table, and, "Because it'll make you happy," Jack said, we walked into the neighborhood church's sanctuary.

So that we could slip out unnoticed at the end of the service, we sat in the back. People dotted pews that were indecent in their emptiness and spread coats and Bibles beside them. They turned to hymn number seventy-four, all four verses, but weren't able to fill the vacuity with their voices. The minister read from the Bible, sending his voice down the aisle as ministers had done in that sanctuary for decades.

Immediately following the benediction, middle and side pew people grouped around us, too eagerly giving too many names and asking too many questions. We edged toward the door, wearing manikin smiles.

Outside, we relaxed in the familiarity of Lexington Avenue buses and dark-suited men drinking egg cream in the candy store and vowed not to return to the church again.

But we did return one more time—on a Good Friday.

A sheet of paper was circulated among employees in my office: "Sign your name if you will be attending church this afternoon. Those who do may leave the office at 1:00 P.M."

I signed. Get the afternoon off with pay? Why not?

We talked over the possibilities: "What'll we do? Go to Central Park? To a movie?"

"The original silent film version of *The Ten Commandments* is playing at the church we went to once," I told Jack.

"Ever seen it?"

"Nope."

"It's a film classic," he told me.

We'd go. The film would be shown in the church basement so we really wouldn't be "going to church." We'd sit in the rear and leave early if we wanted to. Darkness would provide anonymity.

The basement room was crossless and organless. I could imagine coal piled in a corner bin and a bare light bulb hanging from the ceiling. Each folding chair sat separate from its neighbor. No arm around shoulder. Intimacy was severed.

On the day of the cross we sat in stark darkness, forced to examine our God doubts. No cups of soda pop from a lobby refreshment stand to wash down each scene, to dilute H. B. Warner's portrayal of Jesus Christ.

Across town, boys pushed racks of $25.95 cocktail
dresses down garment district streets. Pickpockets worked
Times Square. Taxi drivers cursed their way uptown.
Upstairs, the stained glass sanctuary waited for Sunday.
Downstairs, Jack and I faced a subtitled Jesus Christ
who should have been as out-of-date as the old, scratched
film. Why, then, did I feel as though he were intruding
on our present?

Friends came to our apartment on Friday or Saturday
evenings, freed from their own Monday to Friday nine to
five. We sat on the floor, legs tucked underneath,
metropolitan sages eager to be heard, and talked into a
semidarkened room lit only by a candle set in a bottle
coated with rivulets of multicolored wax. We sipped just
enough wine to coat our minds with bravado.

Jews, Roman Catholics, and Protestants, most of us
were adults who had outgrown childhood religion.
Inevitably, someone would mention God's name.

"God is an invention of man's mind. Man needs the
idea of God."

"What do you mean when you say 'God' anyway?
The name has as many connotations as there are people."

"I believe that there is a God."

"God who? Which God is the real one—if there is a
God at all?"

"Life is unexplainable without God—no beginning."

"Well, if there really is a God, how can he let things
go on in the world as they are? I don't want anything to
do with a God like that!"

"God was my grandmother's invention."

Our glasses were refilled. The room became silent.

"Have you seen the movie at the Paramount? It was
really great. The stage show wasn't so hot, but that
movie . . . ."

Apartment number 45 turned off the radio, put out
the lights, and went to bed. Apartment number 47 put on

a pot of coffee and spread the *New York Times* out on the kitchen table. Our candle burned lower, its wax dripping a new layer on top of the old blues, yellows, reds, and greens. We talked about movies and marriages and money and left God for another Friday or Saturday night. I was glad that the room was dark, because it hid my shame at not having defended him well. He *was* out there, beyond cement, skyscrapers, and farmhouses—somewhere.

Five/ DADDY

The Long Island Railroad train roared into Pennsylvania station and emptied itself of shoppers who'd come to Manhattan for a day at Macy's and Lord & Taylor's and of commuters who came in every weekday to sit at desks heavy with bulging "IN" baskets. They streamed out of the gate past us into the waiting room toward exit and coffee shop signs. Jack and I followed the line of people ahead of us into an empty train car.

"You take the window seat," Jack offered. I slid in and arranged my jacket behind me. He took my left hand in his.

"Let's take off our wedding rings now."

I nodded and we removed our gold bands. He gave his to me, and I dropped them both in my black change purse with nickels, dimes, and quarters.

"First time I've had mine off," he said, rubbing the empty place on his finger.

"Me too." There was no telltale band of whitened flesh where the rings had been as there would be years later.

We'd promised never to take off our wedding rings and now less than a year later they lay with small change in my pocketbook. But we were on our way to visit Daddy in the hospital. Even though our wedding announcements had read: "Mr. Isadore Siegel announces the marriage of his daughter Marion . . .," Daddy didn't know that I was married. Daddy didn't know that mother was dead. Did he know that the world had fought another war? That an end-of-the-world bomb had been invented? For nearly twenty years Daddy had sat slumped and silent in chairs during the day and lay on his bed drifting from silent wakefulness into silent sleep at night. It seemed best to leave death and marriage outside the hospital door.

We settled back in the stiff pile seats that reminded me of Grandma's parlor sofa and watched station platforms approach and vanish. Jack's voice was soft as he pointed out dogs chasing their tails in front yards and queer, crooked, fairy tale houses.

"Tick—ets . . . ."The conductor slid over the word, leaving it to hang in midair and float down the car. He punched our tickets and tucked them in our seats, signs to let him know that our Long Island trip was paid for. At the end of the car, he opened the door, went through it, and closed it behind him.

Our train sped past gated crossings with cars lined on both sides, past little boys on bikes who waved as the train cars flashed by, past the First Methodist Church and the Shopwell Market toward a government-owned institution swathed in country green.

I'd shed marital identity with my gold band. Though Jack and I shared a city apartment and a marriage bed, now he was a stranger. On that Sunday afternoon, there was only Marion Siegel, poverty, Jewishness, and Daddy in the hospital.

On another Sunday ten years before, Mother had packed sandwiches, deviled eggs, and a white cake with chocolate frosting in a brown grocery bag—lunch to share with Daddy. She put on the rust-colored suit she'd taken apart seam by seam and then resewn faded side in. I wore a made-over woman's blue and tan plaid woolen suit.

After a train ride, we stood in the dusty rural depot. Mother spotted the aging green bus and walked around to its front to check the sign: *Veteran's Hospital.* The seat wooshed as we sat down on it, and I pressed my bare legs against it to feel its cold leathery smoothness.

The road wound past white houses with straw-hatted men and women who were bent in their gardens, past a man in striped overalls who was taking mail from a silver mailbox at the roadside. Mother moved the lunch farther back on the seat and stood to open our window from the top. She squeezed the levers together and pushed. The window, sealed to protect beauty shop hairdos, wouldn't budge. A man sitting in the seat in front of us, on his way to visit a son or an old army buddy, stood up and pushed on our window. The muscles on his forearm tightened. "No use," he grunted, redfaced. "They probably haven't been opened since year one."

Our bus pulled into hospital grounds, winding through closely mown green lawns with benches spaced at isolated intervals. Time to play my game: patient, worker, or visitor. The first man was easy because he sat like Daddy: shoulders slumped, chin on chest. Next was a worker. Easy, too, because he wore a white uniform. He didn't count. Two men walked together. Patient and visitor? Two visitors? Two doctors? Probably a patient and his very best friend from the city who was visiting him for the day.

The bus parked in front of the administration office and we walked the short distance to Daddy's building, past what Mother called "the bad ward," where men stood on several-storied, heavily barred porches and screamed about Mr. Roosevelt and the twenty-fifth batallion.

In Daddy's building, Mother and I followed a white-coated attendant, waiting at each door for him to select a key from his oversized ring, turn it in the lock, and lead us into insanity's halls.

We found Daddy sitting in a wooden chair along the wall next to the open door in the dayroom, his shoulders slumped, his chin on his chest, his eyes shut—one of a row of silent patients.

"Hello, Joe," Mother said, bending and kissing him on the cheek and using the given name he'd adopted years ago to avoid Isadore-prejudice. He lifted his head and spoke. "Uh. Hello." Head slowly fell, chin urgently seeking its familiar resting place.

"Joe. Look who's here. It's Marion."

He lifted his head again, slowly.

"Uh. Marion. Yeah." Head slowly fell again.

"Joe, come on, let's move over to the table. We can all sit down and talk." She took his arm and led him to one of several tables in the room. "Here. Let's sit here. I'll sit beside you. Marion, you sit across from your father where you can talk to him."

We slid our chairs up to the table and Mother set the lunch she'd been carrying in front of Daddy. "Look what I brought today. Lunch. See? Cheese sandwiches. You always like cheese sandwiches. Want one?"

Without looking up, he grunted. "Uh. Yeah."

Mother served the Siegel family lunch while a woman at a table behind her placed fried chicken in front of her patient-son. In another part of the room, an older man talked in low tones to a young one who wouldn't answer.

"Marion is studying French in school now." She turned to me. "Get him to talk French to you."

"Daddy?" I spoke loudly to him as Mother always did, calling to the father hidden in the man who sat slumped across from me.

"Daddy? Say something in French to me and see if I can understand you."

He raised his head and struggled to focus on me. "French? Uh. Yeah. French. *Parlez-vous francais?*"

"*Oui, Papa,*" I answered. "*Je parle francais un peu.*"

"*Tres bien.* Very good." A smile pushed at his cheeks. Daddy and I bit into our sandwiches; Mother devoured his smile for her lunch.

"French is nasal," he went on, working to shake off a dozen-year sleep. "We speak it through the nose. Yeah. French words have to come out here." He pointed to his nose and shook with laughter. He looked at his wife. "Through the nose." *"When he was well, your Daddy would do anything to make people laugh,"* Mother had told me often. *"He liked to see people laughing and happy."* Now the Siegel family at lunch giggled at his joke: words pouring through a nose.

"Porte; door. *Chaise;* chair. *Tête;* head," he recited, eager to explore a subject that had never caused him pain. An attendant, who had been leaning against one wall watching, walked over to us. "Mrs. Siegel?"

"Yes?"

"Can I see you for a minute?"

"Ouvrez la porte," Daddy was saying to me.

A few paces behind me, the attendant whispered to Mother. "Does he always talk to you like this when you come?"

"Yes, he always does."

"Amazing. Absolutely amazing. I didn't know he could talk. He never does to us. Never."

"German is another language," Daddy was telling me. "Spoken in the throat." He made a gargling sound and laughed again. Mother sat down beside him and put her hand on his arm.

The conductor slid the car door open and called out an indistinguishable town. Jack consulted our timetable.

"You'd never know it by listening to him, but our stop is next."

The dusty depot. The waiting bus. Mothers carrying offerings of baked ham and apple pie. Fathers who'd fixed the roof on Saturday on their way to visit their sons on Sunday. Wives wearing pink and yellow for their stranger-husbands.

Up winding roads past white houses to hospital grounds. Administration office. Last stop. Jack and I walked to Daddy's building, passing men in other buildings who stood staring through bars in a drug-induced hush. In Daddy's building, an attendant unlocked doors with a key from his oversized ring and led us to the dayroom.

Daddy was sitting in a chair against the wall, his head slumped, his chin resting on his chest.

"Daddy. Hello, Daddy. It's me—Marion." I touched his arm and slowly he raised his head. Without looking at me, he answered. "Uh. Marion."

"Daddy? This is Jack. Jack, this is my father."

My father nodded slightly without looking up.

"I'm glad to see you, Daddy. You look as though you've been eating well. Doesn't he look like the food agrees with him, Jack?"

"He sure does. Mr. Siegel, I'm from New York City. Marion tells me that you know a lot about New York. That right?"

He raised his head slowly, working to shake off a twenty-year sleep. "Uh. New York. Yeah. I know New York."

"Ever been to Chinatown, Mr. Siegel?"

"Chinatown is downtown. You go there by trolley car. A nickel for the ride . . ." Daddy began.

I took my father gently by the arm and led him to a table in the center of the room where we could sit together.

"In Chinatown they have special grocery stores with food from China . . . ."

Our wedding rings lay quietly in their hiding places, careful not to clink against the nickels, dimes, and quarters. Duckworth had become Siegel.

Six/ MOTHERHOOD

Before dawn, the contractions began. I lay beside my sleeping husband in our new Queens apartment timing pains by the luminous hands on our alarm clock. A squeezing pain, promise of birth. The baby who'd grown from speck-like sperm and ovum to full-formed fetus rested for five minutes and gathered strength for the journey down the birth canal into the hands of a Manhattan obstetrician at New York Hospital.

Pain, rest; pain, rest. Hours on floor mats at natural childbirth classes had prepared me for labor. We mothers-to-be had lain in parallel rows practicing labor behavior and comparing child-filled wombs and backaches. We were women preparing for star performances.

For nine months, the life that Jack and I created had been hidden within my body, growing in cradled privacy beneath navy smocks and jumpers with elasticized waists. Our son, when only inches long, had begun reorganizing our lives. Because of him, my stomach had refused cornflakes and hamburgers and demanded only bland white turkey meat.

Light would soon break over New York Hospital. I breathed slowly and deeply as a contraction pushed at my child. When the pain ended, I touched Jack's arm.

He'd been sleeping with impending birth. "Huh? Wha . . . what? Pains? Time?"

"Pains. Every five minutes."

He followed our detailed preplanning: call the doctor from a subway station phone booth (open twenty-four hours) and notify Dave, our neighbor (who'd been ready day and night with shirt and pants over a chair beside his bed) that it was time to drive us to the hospital.

Because birth, determined to keep its divine timetable, pushed relentlessly at our child, Dave roared through near-empty streets that were still silent with sleep, deliberately ignoring red lights. Before morning coffee break, John Lee was born.

Baby John slept in a tiny crib at the foot of my hospital bed in the eight-mother room. Novices, we practiced diapering, feeding, burping, and bathing. Afternoons, we held court, carefully curled and perfumed in after-the-event pink nighties from Bloomingdale's and received our mothers and next-door neighbors. Evenings, hospital-gowned new fathers crowded into the room and handed us bouquets of roses. Later, they sat in bedside chairs shedding junior executive poise as they held their sons and daughters for the first time.

After five days of hospital-launched motherhood, I took our son home to Queens, carrying him in my arms instead of my womb, and laid him in his tiny crib.

Husband and wife; now mother and father.

At birth when the obstetrician placed our infant son on my abdomen, forever severed from womb-life, he presented me with a new self. Sterilizer of bottles. Folder of diapers. Keeper of schedules: six A.M. bottle; nine A.M. cereal; ten A.M. bath; two P.M. bottle; three P.M. walk in the playground; six P.M. feeding.

I immersed myself in motherhood, eager to create an acceptable self-image. Mother was a new self. It was a new image to wear in the park. With wife, it was a new identity to hold up before smirking girlhood memories with the rising and setting of every sun. *This is my husband. Handsome? Sure, he is, but then I'm prejudiced. Yes, Jack and I live in a new apartment building. And this is our baby. Just three months old. I'm a mother. Think of it!*

Two years later, during a scorching New York heat wave, a second son was born. Paul Joseph was a perfect second child. As if to accommodate, he obeyed all the rules: slept four hours between feedings except the one when he quietly explored his crib world. He ate and drank politely and grew at a slow but acceptable pace.

Half-eaten zweibacks on the kitchen floor; a playpen filled with toys in a corner of the living room. The sweet-sour smells of those years enhanced the quality of our lives.

In the suburbs, we invited friends for dinner, drove to Jones' Beach, and took the subway to Macy's. Christmases meant wind-up plush bunnies that played "rock-a-bye-baby," wooden cows that could be pulled across the floor by a string, and fat clowns that tipped over with each push. Thanksgiving dinners were warm family times when everyone smiled, counted blessings, and was glad to be together. I reigned, Queen Mother in a world of immunizations and Little Golden Books.

But yesterday's failures demanded perfection today. Only perfect motherhood could feed my emaciated ego. Pushing and prodding, ego demanded whiter diapers, yet insisted that no diaper was ever white enough. It searched tiny bare bottoms for faint signs of diaper rash. It asked: "Is this banana ripe enough? This bottle clean enough? The tub of water warm enough?"

"Does your baby sit up yet?" a playground mother would ask.

"Not really. He has to be propped up with pillows or he tilts."

"*Really?* My daughter is only five months old and she

sits up by herself. Your baby is six months old, isn't he?''

Another afternoon. "Is your little boy potty trained?''

"Not exactly. Sometimes he . . . .''

"My Robbie is so good. He tells me when he needs to use it now. He's not quite two, you know. Didn't you say that your little boy is past two?''

Back home, ego pushed harder, searching for specks of dirt on the baby dish.

Jack's strength propped up my sagging self; his compliments were breakfast, lunch, and dinner.

"You're a good mother," he'd whisper in my ear as we waited in line in the supermarket. "Thank you for two wonderful sons.''

"Good mother," ego would echo, smacking its lips.

Seeing how worn I was from too much trying, Jack would take over. "I'll sterilize the bottles today," or, "Here. Let me take the diaper pail down to the laundry room. Just give me soap and a clothes basket.''

"Don't worry because he didn't finish his bottle. Think of all the bottles he *has* finished!" he'd assure me. At the end of the day as we sat close together on the couch, he'd wonder aloud. "I don't know how you do it. You take such good care of our sons, keep the apartment clean, cook good meal . . . .'' Ego wolfed his words and sat begging for more.

But ego's appetite wasn't abated. Relentlessly, it sought assurance from motherhood status, from accomplishments, from Jack's words, and from a paperbacked Dr. Spock. Self-confidence was a bleached-out, threadbare garment that left me exposed.

Life seemed to be like hot and cold running water. Thanksgiving today, tragedy tomorrow. Christmas today; crisis tomorrow. Today's joy grayed by tomorrow's threats. And God? He was only a three-lettered attempt at bravado, a golden cross in the front of a sanctuary.

At night, after the boys were asleep, I lay in bed beside Jack.

"Hon?" He'd reach over and take my hand.

"Shh," I'd answer. "I'm praying."

Nearly thirty years old, the only prayers I knew were the ones I'd learned from Mother.

"Our Father who art in heaven; hallowed be thy name . . ."

and

"I lay me down to sleep,
I pray Thee, Lord my soul to keep.
If I should die before I wake,
I pray Thee, Lord, my soul to take."

I was imprisoned in a world of tangibles; veneer bedroom furniture stuffed with underwear and socks in a bedroom next to a kitchen off a bath in a building that crowded against the others beside it. Even the air, thick with smoke and soot, had substance. I searched the corners of our bedroom for some brightness, listened for some sound—a theophany in Queens, New York.

Was God listening?

He must be at home in heaven with his mansion doors shut tight and guarded. The billboards in subway stations say "God so loved the world . . . ." But I'm not the world, I'm only me. What about me? *God, do you hear me?*

I searched for a nod or a handshake from him. In my secret thoughts, I imagined a peaceful place in which healing would pour like the sun's rays. Our family would be together and as we sat on a log, God would speak. "Yes, Marion, I know you. I love you." But there was nothing. Only walls and ceilings and formula to be made and the plumber to call. And uncharted tomorrows. Fear was a chunk of ice in my soul.

God was light years away, a cloistered king, a name at the root of my family tree: *God Almighty, Creator.* As remote as faded tintypes of unidentifiable relatives in an old trunk.

*But will God
actually dwell with
men upon the earth?*
(2 Chron. 6:18).

Seven/ GOD!

Sunday had become our day in parenthesis; our family sanctuary. Ending a long night's fast, Paul would squall from the pit of his stomach until I slipped into a robe and padded into the front bedroom that John Lee and Paul shared with stuffed bears and stick hobby horses. John Lee would be lying on his back in bed "reading" *Puffy, the Puppy* or *The Little Engine That Could.*

Jack, finely tuned to the sounds of fatherhood, would soon answer Paul's hunger pleas, too. One of us would change Paul's diaper, the other sprinkle grains of baby powder on his bare bottom and smooth it in the soft folds of his flesh while the bottle warmed. We'd smile across the crib at one another and breathe deeply of the lives that our love had created.

While Jack went around the corner to the delicatessen for hard rolls and to the candy store for a newspaper, I'd dress and make coffee. Both sons had been fed.

We'd sit at the kitchen table and eat hard rolls spread with cream cheese (topped with smoked salmon when we could afford the luxury). "Dick Tracy's in trouble again," Jack would say, not looking up from the comic section. Then, "Where's Prince Valiant?"

We'd sip our coffee and comment about a Sunday supplement interview, a back page filler. "What's playing at Loews State today?" Jack would ask.

I'd look for the movie section and on my way discover an advertisement for sheets at Gimbel's. We'd linger over the last crumbs, getting up to answer a call from John to "come and see what I made," and plan the rest of our day. The park? A trip to Manhattan?

Years ago under mother-control, Sunday morning meant a leisurely walk past locked dress shops and jewelry stores to church. Now, Sunday was twenty-four hoarded family hours, each one rolled carefully around on the tongue until all that was left was a lingering sweetness that we would taste until the next Sunday brought twenty-four more hours to savor.

We knew, though, that we must do something about our sons and God. Our sons, immunized and vitamined, somehow had to be brought to God's attention. Surely, some black-frocked minister rich in biblical phrases could bring John Lee and Paul to God's attention, penetrating that distant heavenly bastion. Surely, God the Stranger could be wooed and won by parental sincerity, pietistic formality, and childhood innocence.

One Sunday morning, instead of lingering late over Monday ads, I dressed for church. Jack agreed to stay home with the boys.

Downstairs, in front of our building, I had to choose. Which church? Which direction? To the right and around the corner was a red brick church, spread across the block like a fat dowager. To the left and around the corner was a sedate white church. Like a child deciding between two pieces of penny candy, I repeated a childhood rhyme, adding improvisations of my own:

"Eenie, meenie, miney, mo,
In which direction should I go?"

Left won.

The sexton had given the white church its Saturday

night scrubbing and then discreetly donned Sunday
morning invisibility. Lawn grass was nipped at half-inch
height and rid of dandelion blemishes; front steps were
swept clean of secularity, railings relieved of last week's
fingerprints. Congregational dirt clods were vacuumed
from carpeted floors; candy wrappers and old bulletins
penciled with sermon hour notes were ground fine in a
City sanitation truck; pew cushions flattened from the
weight of secret burdens were plumped and made ready
for new ones.

Would the presence of God fall upon the sober
congregation with the first bars of organ music? Was God
the Almighty waiting in the wings for that first prelude
cue, to make his weekly appearance? Would we the people
be rewarded for our church attendance with a glimpse of
him, as a group of loyal subjects is rewarded with a
glimpse of their king at the palace window?

The service kept time to the same denominational
metronome I remembered: a hymn, a prayer, some
Scripture, an anthem, an offering . . . the timeless God's
house routine, reminiscent of church and mother security,
welcomed me back. We the people kept white-gloved
order, wearing our company manners, sitting and
standing, speaking and keeping silent and putting the
weight of our hopes in the hands of the man in the
pulpit.

He was bone slender, as though concerned lest layers
of fat hide his earnestness. His eyes loved. He spoke with
the quiet authority of a man who knew that he was right.
If God had been hidden in a ceiling corner of the
sanctuary and had descended at precisely eleven, his
presence went undetected by me. But the man in the
pulpit seemed to have spent Saturday night with him and
still bore his scent. I left my name and address at the door
and walked home feeling as though tomorow was going to
be Christmas.

During the weeks that followed, Jack and I took turns

going to church and staying home with our sons. Then, escorted by his father, John Lee went, slicked and shining, to Sunday school. Alone for the first time in a world without Mommy, Daddy, or even bedtime bear. Tears puddled down John's cheeks.

"Why don't you stand in the back of the room where he can see you?" teacher-in-charge suggested. "That way he'll sit with the other children at his table, yet still have you for security."

Daddy stayed.

Teacher put a figure on the flannel board. "This poor man was blind," she told the children seated around her in a circle. "He'd never seen the sunshine. He'd never seen his mommy and daddy. Then, one day he met Jesus . . . ." Jack the adult had outgrown nursery-sized tables and chairs, four-line choruses, and primary level Bible stories, but the child within the man had not. That child, weighed with the burden of unanswered questions about God, peered out from behind his adult disguise at a Jesus Christ who healed broken bodies with a touch and whose feet skimmed the surface of the Sea of Galilee. Shamelessly, fervently, the child within hoped for that Jesus to be real, and to be in Queens, New York, on Sunday morning.

The white church around the corner had become my stained glass hope of God. I sat in my Sunday spot while the man in the pulpit introduced Jesus Christ into my secularity. His words gathered around me. "Jesus Christ is the Son of God, divine, just like the Father. Jesus came down to earth from heaven. He demonstrated his divinity by the miracles he performed, and then willingly died as a substitute for you, in order to pay the price that had to be paid for your sins. Because of him, your life can be forever. He loves you; he wants to establish a personal father-child relationship. Believe. Let down your barriers and reach out to him and he will come into your life."

Jesus: foreign proper name, expletive deleted, catchword of tent evangelists and radio preachers. *Jesus:*

alive before Ramses II ruled Egypt and Nebuchadnezzar built the Hanging Gardens? *Jesus:* lover of my soul? Everlasting Lord? I had to determine once and for all who he was.

But cynicism began standing on its hind legs and pawing at me. Cynicism, urbane and sneering, clawed at the message's lack of sophistication, stealing hope as a hawk steals eggs.

"What if he's wrong?" doubt snarled. "You'll make a fool of yourself. This is nothing more than low-intellect religion. Do you want to commit yourself to a God who never shows up? Imagine! Expecting God to bend down and kiss you on the top of the head, to hold your hand and smile at you. He's got a universe to worry about, you know."

But the pastor's words piled up inside me, layer upon layer, and some inner self seemed to be peering at them, lifting them, inspecting them, and running away. Soon, though, that inner self was back again, peering, wondering, and hoping.

The memory of men on street corners who preached a Jesus Christ religion to the accompaniment of snickers, guffaws, and a portable organ flashed on and off like a warning light, and memories of friends' voices warned me that God was AWOL. "Be sensible," I could hear them advise. But the promise that I could know God swelled up inside of me, crowding doubt into a corner.

One Sunday evening after church, I dressed Paul in sleepers and laid him on his stomach in the crib. A bedtime story for John Lee. One last question, one last drink of water, prayers for Mommy, Daddy, Grandma, and Grandpa, the bedtime bear close by, and the routine was complete. Usually then, Jack and I would sit together in the living room searching Sunday night for a last bit of contentment. We'd both take off our shoes; he'd drape his tie over a doorknob. Over coffee, we'd talk about the day and perhaps watch a TV show.

On that Sunday evening, however, I left the boys

settling for sleep and went directly into our own bedroom
and closed the door behind me.

Tomorrow morning, garbage men would empty our
weekend with gloved hands and bury it beneath beer
bottles and empty fried chicken containers down the block.
I'd jump at the jangling alarm, and splash water on my
face. Cook cereal. Fry eggs. Build a block house with John
Lee. Buy milk at the supermarket. Take Jack's suit to the
cleaners. Vacuum and scrub away Sunday. Hide in the
security of the visible and tangible from the unseen,
unknown God.

Tomorrow, I could cloak myself in urgency and hustle
to elude the persisting Jesus questions. Tomorrow was a
cunning figure summoning me to lose myself in him. But
pressed by promises that I could know God, I dropped to
my knees at the foot of the bed and bowed my head. In a
bedroom crowded with manufactured ''Now I lay me's''
and ''Our Fathers,'' I spoke my first words to the missing
God.

''God, I have to know if it's true. If Jesus Christ is
real, if he is divine—if I can know you, then I want to.''

That was all.

I remained kneeling in a soundless, motionless
universe, a thousand years from childhood, from Sunday
school, from mother-trust. Hope, squeezing at my chest,
reached out and felt its way around the universe for God.
Was he there?

He was there.

When I put pride on the floor and knelt on it, God
communicated with me, not in words, but in some silent,
inner fashion—immortal God to mortal man. God wasn't
isolated beyond cement and skyscrapers—beyond some
unfamiliar galaxy. He was here in Queens, New York, on
my block, in my apartment, in my bedroom. Now he was
in my life.

The earth began revolving on its axis again; sounds of
the night resumed. Without seeing, I saw; without

understanding, I knew: Jesus Christ *was* the Son of God. He *had* established a personal relationship with me. Verses that the man in the pulpit had pressed persistently into my mind now spoke: "But to those who did receive Him He granted authority to become God's children, that is, to those who believe in His name" (John 1:12), and "He who has the Son has that life . . . " (1 John 5:12).

The next morning, I stood before the twin tubs in the kitchen taking diapers from hot, sudsy water in the apartment-sized washer, putting them through the wringer, dipping them in cool, clear rinse water and feeding them through the wringer again. Dip, wring, swish, wring. The clank of frying pan against burner and wooden spoon against bowl, the banging of rattle against high chair and the squeaks of a television cartoon mouse. Sensations and sounds of Monday.

This Monday, however, I washed, dried, cooked, and scrubbed, knowing that *God is.* The God who had been locked in hymns and ministerial prayers, a once-a-week phenomenon, had stepped out of his Sunday prison and into my life.

Jesus Christ, Son of God.

No longer was I caged in humanity, unable to uncover a clue to the maddening mystery of Man and God.

Jesus Christ, Son of God.

I shook out the wet, board-stiff diapers as they came through the wringer and put them in the clothes basket.

Jack will know. He'll know that something has happened to me.

I celebrated silently during the next few weeks, waiting for Jack to discover my secret in the same way that he'd discover a surprise dessert in the refrigerator. Unbelievable to me, he didn't seem to notice.

One Sunday, I walked to the front of the sanctuary to announce my infant faith in Jesus Christ publicly. After the service, I went home and told Jack (who'd been minding a sick son) what I'd done. A smile spread across his lips and moved to his eyes (the way he smiled when he said "I love you"); he took my hand and squeezed it and said, "I'm glad."

On another Sunday about three months later, Jack went to church alone. Soon after noontime, he came through the front door. On the way to the bedroom to rid himself of coat and tie, he kissed me and handed me the church bulletin.

"Ready to eat," I called in a few minutes from the kitchen.

We four settled at the table. I began to cut Paul's meat into pieces and put it into his dish. John Duckworth, agnostic, turned to me and spoke three words.

"I believe now."

I hugged him with my words from across the table, careful of fragile new faith. We played airplane with spoonfuls of mashed potatoes as we fed Paul. We passed the butter and refilled our glasses and pretended that this was only a summer Sunday afternoon, but our eyes met between forkfuls and joy spilled across our faces.

Spirit birth; touch of God.

Eight/ MISSIONARIES

Before Spirit birth, I'd been like a creature running on a maze trail, separated from the millions of others running on their own trails. Each of us had been plunked down unceremoniously at START HERE and would run wildly until we came to DEAD END.

Now I'd stepped out of the maze into a world whose beginning and end was God. Life seemed broader and higher than it had ever been. It reached beyond the lady upstairs who taught me how to make soup from chicken backs and necks, out past the neighbor who repaired TV sets, beyond Skyscraper City, down rural roads . . . . The world was God's idea. Grass was green and trees budded, leafed, dropped their leaves, and budded again because he'd made it so.

God was the answer in the back of the book, but ego was still my resident master. Ego still shook old skeletons and held up Siegel like a pack of incriminating letters. Ego still sat in the center of my soul and handed down evaluations, set goals, issued orders, blackmailing me with yesterday.

God was my promise of eternal life. He was divinity resting quietly in my spirit, available for twenty-four-hour consultation. I allowed him to help me cope with midnight baby fevers and unexplained crying sessions—to straighten and dust the surface of my life like a live-in housekeeper, but I kept yesterday's hurts locked up and off-limits, fearful that God's handling of them would cause fresh bleeding, new pain. Masked in pseudo-identities, I skimmed the surface of life not daring to look beneath at the self I hated.

I continued to immerse myself in my mother role. With neighborhood mothers, I stepped out of our front door each afternoon as though performing a ritual. We walked to a cluster of stores together where we bought bananas to mash for our babies' suppers, picking through the yellow ones to find ones properly flecked with brown. In the butcher shop, in the candy store, we advised one another and wished well. We bought our children dixie cups and held their hands when they crossed the streets. When supper hour threatened, we said goodbye, see you tomorrow unless it rains. I pushed the carriage toward home, glad that Betty from down the block and Mitzie from around the corner knew only "mother" me, and not the "real" me.

I prayed that, in the midst of the mother talk, I might have an opportunity to tell them how they could find God. A neighbor with whom I exchanged baby-sitting and tips on how to remove stains, accepted my invitation to hear Billy Graham speak in Madison Square Garden. At the end of the message, she rose and walked down to the platform. While I waited, she prayed with a counselor and asked the Jesus to whom she'd curtsied every Sunday morning to come into her life.

Jack and I shook hands with new experiences like people in a reception line. I stood before a roomful of twelve-year-olds and told Bible stories still new to me, struggling with ancient, unfamiliar names like "Mephibosheth." At midweek service, I spoke a sentence prayer out loud, a simple, childish thing flanked on both

sides by the impressively correct-sounding prayers of
veterans that had been constructed according to some
master pattern. My voice was thin and shaking, and my
words seemed to have been chosen from a first-grade
reader, but I'd spoken with God in the presence of others
and I knew that he was a proud Father.

Now Jack and I found ourselves wanting something
more than we wanted a new living room rug or a house in
the country. We wanted to caress people for God. Before
Spirit birth, subway crowds had been a heaving mass of
strangers with their heads buried in the *News* or *Times*,
fighting us for seats, pushing us out of the way as they
headed for the door. They'd been uptown traveling
downtown; downtown traveling uptown. They'd climbed
Queens BMT and IRT subway stairs and headed for their
own houses where they mowed snippets of grass and
pruned precious trees. They waited at red lights like dogs
straining on leashes. They were THEY, a million-count
rising and falling tide in which Jack and I swam, clinging
together. Now, though, they were painted and tailored
Hansels and Gretels without a trail of crumbs to follow.
And now, we knew the way.

To Jack, eight hours at a desk routing shipments in
exchange for dollars to pay bills to sustain life was self-
defeating. If the name on his office door were painted over
and the desks, chairs, filing cabinets, and typewriters sold,
if the phone company disconnected each extension, New
Yorkers would push their way to the subways as they
always had and divert anxiety's attention with the comics.
Salvaged evening and weekend hours were the important
ones. Then Jack could visit men huddled in their secret
miseries in airshaft furnished rooms and elevator
apartments; he could visit the Bowery Mission and linger
to talk God with those whose hunger went deeper than
their stomachs.

It wasn't enough anymore to belong to one another in
a city bereft of "How are ya's." It wasn't enough to be

able to say "Two, please," at the box office or to be
known by the landlord as "they." We weren't satisfied
any longer to fold protectively into one another in our
Queens apartment.

We asked God to show us how we could serve him
with our lives. While we waited, Jack studied the Bible
and prepared himself for a ministry.

At a dinner sponsored by a Christian organization,
we learned of an interdenominational home missionary
organization that supplied pastors to rural communities.
These pastors and their wives opened closed churches and
supplied leadership to communities that had none. They
visited in farm homes on unnamed dirt roads and talked
about the price of chicken feed and prayed silently for a
chance to talk about God. Some communities were in lush
midwestern farm country; others in parched California
desert; still others in western logging country.

Rural home missionaries? A tiny church on a back
road with a bell to ring every Sunday morning? A few
square miles of hills and valleys assigned to John and
Marion Duckworth by God himself?

One evening after dinner we took the application that
the mission had given us from its drawer and waded
through mothers' maiden names and birth dates. We
stamped our future and dropped it in a mailbox.

The mailman brought letters from friends and
relatives, bills, dozens of envelopes marked "Occupant,"
magazines, advertisements that began "prices
slashed—must sell," and finally a letter from the
missionary society. "You have been accepted . . . ."

Accepted!

Accepted to stand in the pulpit of a tiny church with
loose shingles and chipped paint, or on the stage of a
community hall flanked by a choir seated on folding chairs
facing a congregation seated where Saturday night square
dances had been held! We'd leave Queens, New York,
leave our families, our friends, for *somewhere* . . . .

Somewhere, our mission board wrote, was a town nestled as close to the west coast as New York City was to the east. *Somewhere* couldn't be found on our gas station road map. We finally found it printed in miniscule type in a hard-backed, carefully precise atlas.

We began sifting through our lives. "My mother crocheted these doilies," I told Jack as I sorted through the linen closet, adding to the two growing piles of "keep" and "sell or give away." "They sat on the back and arms of the old morris chair and kept sliding around until she finally held them in place with pins. They go with us."

Picture albums. Me at five sitting on the front porch of our house holding my larger-than-life-sized new doll. Jack on the beach baring his thirteen-year-old chest. Me in Washington, D.C., in front of the Lincoln Memorial.

Jack's Boy Scout uniform and merit badges; his Grandpa's hunting jacket—the one that he'd worn to national trap shoot meets where he was nearly always a prizewinner. Bedtime bear. Moo cow. Puppy, Paul's pink, stuffed, eyeless treasure. Blocks, puzzles, trucks, and cars. Bedtime story books in whose peanut-butter-smeared pages lived steam shovels and pancakes that could talk and whose friendships were as real as the little girl's down the block. A green carriage cover knitted by Grandma.

The top of our wedding cake. The glass-topped coffee table that had held nine years of coffee cups and five years of baby bottles. Save; go. Must keep; give away or sell.

Self-hatred was another "must keep." It was closeted within me like an idiot child whose identity I refused to own. My subconscious idea about my real self was as much a part of my sense of personhood as my name. No surgery was delicate enough to separate me from self-hatred. Lodged within the mystery of my mind, it would travel west.

Nine/ WEST

Nothing in New York City had prepared me for the West, for its miles of tree-covered mountains swept into expansive valleys. We stopped at the side of the road and stood holding hands at the edge of an evergreen-coated cliff that plunged hundreds of feet below, mute at the otherworldliness of it

We drove on, following a winding road squeezed between a rocky cliff and the seashore and, before we crossed a bridge over an Indian-named river, just a few miles outside of the new community that would be home, we stopped to tuck in shirttails and wash sticky hands and faces.

The proprietor of the general store, who was sorting mail behind a U.S. Post Office sign (separated by stamps and mailboxes from the displays of flannel shirts and cornflakes), gave country-clear directions. "Down the road, make a left, go to the top of the hill, turn at a dirt road on the left going into the woods."

Down the road, left, top of the hill, left, a dirt road interruption in the acres of firs and pines, into a clearing and we pulled up in front of the home we'd traveled 3000 miles to see—a tiny red cabin in the woods.

"I'll get the big suitcase," Jack yelled on the way back to the car after a first inspection. We were home. At motel stops, we'd brought in only an overnight case containing pairs of pajamas, toilet articles, coloring books and crayons, and changes of clothing.

Home.

We'd put Rockefeller Center and hard rolls from the delicatessen behind us; we'd become westerners with mud on our boots and an axe in our hands.

Our four-room cabin, the largest of a cluster of weekend hunting cabins in the fairy tale forest clearing, was the only empty house in town. No one had ever lived there all winter before.

All the buildings had been painted red: the cabins, the smokehouse (a sign over its door read, "This isn't it"), the outhouse (a sign over *its* door read, "This is it"). Moss, like scraggly green-gray beards, hung from solemn old-men trees that ringed the clearing.

Services that had been provided with the signing of a lease were up to us now. *There,* water poured from faucets—hot as well as cold. *Here,* water was supplied by a creek hidden in the woods, pumped uphill by a ram jet pump, and piped into a fifty-gallon oil drum that stood on a platform not far from the cabin. From there, it was piped into the doll-sized kitchen sink where it ran out—cold. Daily, Jack took the path to trip the ram, to fill the tank to pipe the water into the house until the temperature dropped and the pipes froze. Then, he made daily trips to the general store to fill milk cans with water instead of into the hills to trip the ram.

Here, baths were Saturday night events. Water was heated and, after dinner, we brought the round tin tub in from the back porch. After John Lee and Paul had bathed and been put to bed, Jack and I took turns sitting yoga fashion and splashing in four inches of water.

There, heat filled the rooms with the flick of a thermostat. *Here,* heat was dispensed by a potbellied stove

that devoured wood like a starving animal. Jack ran a
weary trail between woodpile and wood box. Living room
temperature alternated between long underwear and fan.

There, animals had been confined to Central Park
where they entertained us on Sunday afternoon. *Here,*
animals roamed freely, sharing the Northwest country with
us. Deer tiptoed through the woods and ventured across
the road after dark. Herds of elk came down from the
mountains and fed in open fields. With field glasses, we
picked out goats on mountainsides. Bears ventured into
apple orchards in the fall, gorging themselves on Golden
Delicious.

There, we read the weather report each evening in the
Daily News and planned what to wear the next morning.
Here, there was no need. The sky was always gray and
heavy with rain; the ground always wet, the old-men trees
always dripping from their mossy beards. I innocently
asked a woman in the community when I first arrived:
"When is the rainy season?" She laughed. "Let me put it
this way. The sun shines in July and August. Sometimes."

I hung clothes out to dry in a clearing in the woods
during the weeks after I arrived. They hung there day after
day, dripping. Finally, we strung clotheslines across the
living room and ducked wet pant legs in the face.

In New York, someone else was sitting on my gray
sofa, someone else was polishing my glass-topped coffee
table, drinking out of my cups, eating out of dishes I'd
had to leave behind in my other life.

Here in the Northwest, I was proving my self-worth
through sacrifice. A rural missionary. No water, no
bathroom, no thermostatically controlled heat, no tiled
floors or formica countertops, no basement laundromat or
corner bus. Now, we were Pastor and Mrs.; surely, now I
wasn't Marion Duckworth née Siegel of the Jewish Siegels
of welfare and insanity. Surely, now I'd be able to like
myself.

I fantasized to girlhood acquaintances-turned-matrons

as I folded clean laundry and as I lay in bed at night.

Hi. Good to see you. What are we doing? Well, you see my husband is a minister. He pastors rural churches that can't afford leadership. Obeying God is more important to us than making money.

Yes, the Northwest is fabulous. Plenty of game. Fishing. Backpacking in the mountains. We pick up oysters on the beach a couple of miles from the house. Game in the woods. Yes, it is a kind of utopia, isn't it? Everything we could want. Things have turned out well for me, haven't they?

They'd like me now. I wasn't the person they'd known me to be any longer. I wasn't . . . I wasn't . . . .

We moved from the red cabin in the woods to a larger house on a hundred-acre ranch on the river. In the front yard of the new parsonage, John Lee and Paul played under low hanging pines and stirred mud ice cream with pine needle sprinkles in tin can dishes. On warm days, we packed picnic lunches and sat on the bank of the river that ran just behind the ranch, and listened to the water splash its way down from the mountains. After we'd eaten, we studied bear tracks that led from the muddy riverbanks into the woods. Mountains ringed themselves solidly around us as if appointed by God. We sat in their shadow at night watching porcelain deer munch apples in the orchard.

The church congregation grew from six to sixty. With the men and women in the community, we built a log church on a hill and hung a bell to ring in its tower. Groups of young people listened as we told them about the God we'd discovered in New York City. Some spilled out words to him: "I want to know you, God. Jesus Christ, are you there?" Loggers, their wives, and children drove up the hill to the church and filled the pews on Sunday. "God," they breathed in long-held-back sighs. And then, "My God?" Finally, they spoke the words in firm, sure voices: *"My God."* A logger began to carry his

New Testament into the north woods with him and read it
while he ate his lunch. An octogenarian took communion
for the first time. A schoolteacher closed her book on
evolution and opened her Bible.

In spite of full-time worker status, self-hatred insisted
that someone like me could never really be a God-pleasing
Christian. I felt a vague sense of guilt about myself, and
didn't know what to do about it. On Monday, washday, I
searched for answers.

A wringer-style washing machine with tin tubs on an
enclosed porch with mildew growing on the damp walls
was my laundromat. Water from faucets through a hose
into the washer. A load of sheets. Soap. Switch on.

I sat on a kitchen chair next to a table loaded with
books and Bibles while the washer churned. Surrounded
by boxes of apples, sacks of potatoes, piles of squash and
pumpkins, toy dump trucks, a wagon, hip boots, and
fishing poles, I read: "If, then, you have been raised with
Christ, seek the things which are above, where Christ is
seated at God's right hand. Apply your mind to things
above, not to things on earth; . . . put to death whatever
in your nature belongs to the earth . . ." (Col. 3:1, 2, 5a).

"Put to death . . ." the washer churned out as the
soap worked deeper into mud-caked pants. Saint Paul
frowned at me in apostolic censure. I wedged the centuries
between us and hid behind them. How could I obey the
hard, black, demanding Bible words? How could I become
an always humble inside-and-out saint-in-the-flesh like the
full-time Christian ladies powdered with peace, with
unselfishness combed through their hair?

Books. *Absolute Surrender. Meet for the Master's Use.*
Each a front-of-the-room teacher demanding to be obeyed.

Unload washer. Clothes through wringer into first
tub. Reload washer. Read another book. Search for some
secret grow-quick formula.

By late afternoon, the washer and tubs had been
drained and wiped dry for another Monday. I stacked my

Bibles and books and slid them back into their places in the bookcase. With guilt still dragging at my coattails, I hung up the last batch of wet clothes and went to the kitchen to start supper.

Ten/ IDENTITY

Our next church, during its hundred-year existence, had
been open and closed, pastored and pastorless.
Congregations had sat in its pews and waited for a minister
from town to come and preach. They'd sung hymns and
waited in silence, sung again, waited again, and looked
back over their shoulders at a door that didn't open.
Finally, they buttoned their coats around their hungry
souls and went home.

The community, an RFD route without gas station or
general store, was a Grandma Moses mural with "places"
painted in—a house, a barn, a garden plot, perhaps a cow,
chickens, some sheep, a horse. Fruit trees. At least one
dog, usually a collie. The scene also included split-levels
built by families in flight from town.

The parsonage was a two-bedroom cottage suitable for
a Mr., a Mrs., and their miniature poodle, but not for a
family of four when one member is a minister with
bulging files and hundreds of books. When a third son,
nine-pound Mark, was born and moved in with his crib,
bathinette, playpen, and high chair, I had to sidle
between the bed, crib, and dresser like a customer in a
used furniture store

A desk, sized for an executive suite, spread itself like a domineering mother-in-law across the tiny living room. Fat with forms for me to make out and lessons for me to do, it eyed me critically, flanked and supported by its imposing friends, the four-drawer filing cabinet and the floor-to-ceiling bookcase.

The round kitchen table was never empty. It was piled with laundry, set with dishes for a meal, littered with dirty dishes from a meal, covered with bags of groceries to be put away, strewn with Bibles and notebooks for a Bible class. Across from the table, the bathinette hovered in a corner pushed against the wall by the washing machine which was crowded by the dryer which was wedged against the sink.

One cleaning day, I hauled stacks of toys from the empty spaces in which they were stuffed in the boys' room. *Move this from here to there and back to here again.* I got down on my hands and knees and began pulling shoes, boots, sagging cardboard toy boxes, and trucks out from under the bed, then I flattened, belly on floor, to reach a toy car that lurked in a corner against the wall. Inevitably, I raised up too soon and smashed my back against the bed railing. I jerked back in pain and banged my elbow against the dresser just inches behind me.

"I hate this house. I hate it. I hate it. It isn't fair that I have to put up with these circumstances," I stormed silently, rubbing my elbow and mourning for the pain in my back that I couldn't reach. I shoved toys and shoes back under the bed and pushed the guilt over my resentfulness into the back of my mind where it found rejection and inadequacy for its companions.

Guilt was a nagging live-in relative that I kept hidden. Guilt over my inner feelings seemed to have spread until it infested all of me. It followed after me, shaking an accusing finger until every minor misstep seemed major. *You may fool others into thinking that*

you're a model Christian, but we know better, don't we?
You're egocentric. You're full of self-pity. You can't obey
the Scripture you teach.

Mid-morning while Mark slept, I collected Bible and
prayer list and, when the weather was warm, sidled
between bookcase, playpen, and desk, went out the front
door, and sat on the step.

Guilt demanded perfect devotions. It pressed leaden
against my soul with displeasure when morning Bible
reading didn't culminate with a flash of insight and it
branded that time with God: *failure.* Prayer must be
perfect intercession; each name, each situation, each day.
Personal prayer had deteriorated to mechanical "up and
down the notebook pages" procedure, punctuated with
wordless moans to God.

Beyond the cottage, a doe and her fawn lay in their
own secret place curled up in the morning warm. A
farmer's wife pours coffee into cups. Out of the kitchen
window, she watches her men dismount tractors, climb out
of pickups. A PTA calendar hung on the kitchen wall:
"Grange dinner 6:00. Bring potato salad and pie. Friday,
town. Sunday, church potluck."

A bride and groom photograph in a gold frame on
the dresser. A granny-square afghan made by her mother
at the foot of the bed. The tiny elephant figures she
collects on shelves over the fireplace in the living room.
Her house is the Melville place. She is Ginny who has a
way with African violets—who tends to be overweight, and
confesses to too many cinnamon rolls with her morning
coffee.

Women like Ginny Melville dotted the countryside.
They seemed satisfied with and secure in their identity.
They seemed to like themselves. Local high school.
College. A white fluff marriage recorded in The Wedding
Book. House. Children. The Ginny Melvilles were
Christians, but they were excused from minister's wife
perfection by a God who took note of their secularity.
They could alibi quick tempers and extra fat and speak

vaguely over coffee about "needing God's help."

Mrs. Minister's wife, I was sure, was called to spiritual superiority. The growing collection of deeper Christian life books on our public library-sized living room bookshelves—hardback and paperbacked, theological and devotional—taught and preached victory. A total commitment; a flash of God-given insight. I continued to probe them and hoped for a seeing at last when I'd be transformed into a supersaint Christian leader instead of one who bit her fingernails and bathed her soul-wounds in self-pity.

My search for a magic-grow formula intensified as the pressure for a perfectionist kind of Christian life increased. I began each new book expectantly. I dreaded THE END when the author had no more to say to me. I submitted to God again. I squeezed my eyes shut tightly and pushed out each word of my prayer. "God, I want to get rid of myself. I want Jesus Christ to control me. Make it happen, Lord. Please? Reduce me to nothing. *You* fill me instead."

Why didn't it happen? Why couldn't I duplicate the author's experiences—see myself as a wholly new person who wanted nothing to do with self-centeredness? Why couldn't I become a "nothing" so that God could control me? Wasn't that what he wanted to do?

One Monday, Jack and I locked the cottage door behind us, fastened Mark in his car seat, and drove out of the driveway. It was a day off—that day of the week when Pastor shed pulpit and pew and became friends with himself again. This Monday, we wouldn't go shopping as we usually did, running from store to store and crossing items off our list. Instead, we'd take a long drive and stop for lunch.

As we drove, we left pieces of the work week scattered behind us like strewn garments.

". . . Sunday school contest. Three weeks to go. I wonder if we'll . . . ."

". . . Got to go to the hospital and visit tomorrow

morning for sure. Surgery for Mrs. . . ."

"Must remember to buy stencils when we go to the
store . . . ."

"Monthly reports this week. I'll get the figures
ready . . . ."

As signposts noted passing miles, "We'll have to get
the church furnace fixed this week," gave way to, "Hey,
look, a New Jersey license plate." We exchanged
conversational exclamation marks. "Look at that field of
corn! It really is as high as an elephant's eye." "Mark,
look at the nanny goat in the yard." We were becoming
Monday tourists as we drove past unfamiliar houses with
sleeping dogs on their front porches. The pastoral burden
slipped from our shoulders and lay on the back seat ready
to be assumed on Tuesday.

Trivia paved the way for substance. Mark fell asleep in
the car seat, and Jack and I talked about his fat red
cheeks, the thumb in his mouth, "blanket" clutched in
his other hand. We reviewed the cardboard carton robot
that John Lee was building at home and the blue cowboy
shirt with pearl buttons that Paul had saved Christmas and
birthday gift money to buy. We talked about God,
ourselves, and God and ourselves.

Because the one gas station, one store towns we drove
through kept their own Monday rhythm, discreetly
ignoring me, I began to verbalize some of the question
marks within. "Does God want us to lose our
personality—our own individuality so that we can be filled
with his?"

"I don't think he wants us to lose either," Jack told
me. "We all have habits, characteristics, and attitudes that
he wants to change, but God still wants us to remain
ourselves."

"But how can we? Man is totally sinful. Isn't
everything about us evil?"

"Man has an innate tendency to sin. We can't change
that about ourselves. We accept Christ into our lives, and

then need to learn to depend on him to change us, gradually. But because we have a tendency to sin, that doesn't mean we are no good—that we're supposed to get rid of who we are.''

I became silent. *God doesn't want me to lose my personhood? Who am I, anyway? What part of me is acceptable to God? What part does he want to do away with? How can I do his will unless I become a person without a will of my own—a nothing full of God?*

I don't want to be a nothing! I want to be me!

But the only me I could identify was one I hated. That me seemed to have gotten lost in childhood and still seemed to wander like a teenager feeling unacceptable and worthless, expecting rejection to barrel around every corner. That me was like a blown-glass figure; one flick of the finger and she'd shatter. A cross word from Jack, the unrecognizing stare of a casual acquaintance on the street. A frown, a raised eyebrow, a whisper and I withdrew into sulking silence.

If that person is really me, I don't want anything to do with her. I want to get rid of her. Permanently. I want to have a new, acceptable identity.

I pushed my thoughts deep into the back of my mind with others already hidden there. Late that afternoon we drove back to our cottage-parsonage, and in the months that followed, goaded by guilt, I continued to try to satisfy ego by practicing perfectionism, and searched Bible and books to discover how to get rid of the self I hated and to become a nothing person full of God.

Eleven/ EGO

Four years later, we moved to another community that needed a pastor—a miniature America: a mayor, a notary public, schools, one gas station, a general store, a tavern, a post office, a library, a restaurant, a fire station. Civic groups, PTA, and Little League. Nearly all of the men logged. Most worked for The Company; a few owned or worked for gyppos—independent logging operations.

This town wasn't a tourist stop on a well-traveled highway as our first home had been, nor a community a few miles up the hill from the shopping center, as our second home had been. This town was a surprise on a narrow, pasture-and-woods-lined road an hour from doctors and supermarkets where the life style was dominated by logging: pre-dawn treks back into the woods, early evening chores, early bedtime, long, lean periods when weather closed down logging operations.

To a few people, the preacher, his wife, and sons were like members of their own families. To the rest, church was simply a building on a corner. To them, we were "that new preacher and his family" who lived a church-parsonage life.

The parsonage was just a block from the business

section of town. Neighbors' houses lined the streets in all
directions. Here in mini-America, I wasn't safely isolated
from frowning strangers by distance as I'd been in other
communities where houses were acres apart and town miles
away and where, because I didn't drive, Jack and I had
gone everywhere together. Then, I'd depended on him to
build friendship bridges. When they were firmly
established, I knew I could walk across them without fear
of rejection. Here, I was expected to build my own
friendship bridges.

I longed for New York City anonymity.

Afternoon walks to the post office or the general store
were like teenaged walks down Main Street past clusters of
boys and girls from second period English or sixth period
study hall who had stood in front of the Greek's. Then, I
held my breath and studied the sidewalk as I hurried past
and pretended not to see them. I still felt the way I had
when I was a teenager. I wanted to pretend not to see
townspeople who stood buying stamps at general delivery
and who stood on the sidewalk flicking through their mail.
They were people whose names I knew because I'd seen
them at a meeting at school or at a community group
picnic. They were Sunday school dropouts. *Say "hello."
Say "nice day." Say something,* I'd think.

On rare occasions, I'd blurt a "Hi" and flash a
church door smile as I hurried to my post office box.
Usually, though, I'd pretend elaborate preoccupation with
Mark, scurry in the door, and work our combination lock
with the concentration of a mission control engineer at lift-
off minus ten.

At the general store, when I spied in the bread aisle
an unchurched lady to whom I'd once been introduced, I
hurried to the detergent aisle and pretended to read the
boxes. When I was sure she was gone, I crept home sick at
my cowardliness.

On some afternoons, I walked past the post office,
through the town's back streets on some errand. The town,

with its houselined blocks set around a village square, seemed to me to be the grown-up version of a toy village made from a child's "Make-a-Town" set. I was afraid of these mystery houses with the drawn-shade look where those who were not members of the church family lived. A husband, retired from the woods, and his wife. Garden. Flowers. Are they playing cards at the kitchen table? Is he working in a basement shop; is she sewing in the bedroom? I could go to the door and knock. She'd answer. "Hello," I'd say. "I'm Marion Duckworth, the minister's wife. I thought I'd introduce myself." Would she stand inside the screen door unsmiling, speaking in grudging monosyllables and staring at me?

Around the corner, a brown shingled house. A husband, wife, and their three school-aged children. Is she watching a soap opera on TV? Is she talking with her mother on the phone? If I stop, will she come to the door and say, "Sorry, I'm too busy to visit with you," close the door, and leave me standing on the porch with smile running down my face?

"Guilty. *Guilty.*" My stomach churned guilt; my legs turned weak from the weight of guilt as I hurried the back streets for the safety of home. *Next time,* I promised. *Next time I'll be stronger. Next time I'll walk up to the door and knock. I'll be invited inside and we'll drink coffee together and become friends. Next time . . .* But next time was always another last time.

A merry-go-round of church activities provided good works to present to God, to guilt, and to ego. Ego was a peacock, well-hidden behind proper Christian modesty that ruled from his inner throne. "Preside, organize," he ordered. "Chairman. Superintend. Keep that face scrubbed and ready for inspection. Front and center. Work, work."

Empty place where the choir should be? "Marion, how about taking on the job? We *need* a choir director."

"Well, sure, I'll lead the choir." At home, I

practiced directing four-four time from an instruction book
in front of a mirror, fumbling awkwardly in the air. With
one finger, I picked out soprano and alto on the piano and
looked in music books for beats of a quarter note and a
full rest.

"I don't know who is going to be Sunday school
superintendent this year. You'd be good at it, Marion.
You do it. I know you're doing so much already . . . ."

At home, after I practiced as choir director, I prepared
to be Sunday school superintendent. Then, as Bible Club
director, I put together a curriculum, found teachers,
directed the program, and prepared to teach a class. I
organized and prepared to teach Junior Church. I puzzled
over fresh material as youth group sponsor.

At the close of each exhausting day, ego purred.
Soon, though, it stirred again and stalked the confines of
my inner self. "More," it mewed. I got up from my chair
and moved to the bookshelf, to the kitchen counter.
"More," it howled. And obediently, I prepared a lesson,
drew a visual aid, began a newsletter, vacuumed a
rug . . . .

Often, during these super-Christian years, Jack warned
me to slow down. One evening he dug his heels into every
word as he spoke. "What am I going to do with you?
Look at you. You're absolutely exhausted."

The boys were in bed asleep on clean sheets in clean
bedrooms. The house was vacuumed and scrubbed, there
was a freshly baked batch of cinnamon rolls on the kitchen
counter, the drawers were full of clean, folded clothes, my
teaching material was prepared and a list of tomorrow's
tasks ready in my notebook.

I sat across from Jack in the living room like a
flopping, life-sized cloth doll with an embroidered stare on
my face.

"Why do you insist on doing too much? Why won't
you listen to me and slow down? You'd better go to bed
early."

I looked at the floor.

He swallowed a mouthful of frustration and spoke in his "I love you" tone. "I worry about you, honey. Please, please, slow down."

Ego yawned. Fattened on the day's ration of accomplishments, it slept.

3

*Call to Me and
I will answer you . . .*
(Jer. 33:3).

*The Father Himself
loves you . . .*
(John 16:27).

*The Lord disciplines
the person He loves . . .*
(Heb. 12:6).

Twelve/ FAITH

After dragging self-hatred like a dirty childhood bundle
for most of my forty-two years, I threw it against the wall
and shattered the carefully censored parsonage atmosphere
with a prayer-scream: "God help me; I don't know who
I am!"

We'd moved from mini-America to the island
pastorate where our parsonage was a split-level house on
the shore. No red outhouse or ram jet pump. No crowded,
furniture-filled rooms. Here we had hot and cold running
luxury.

But nothing changed the way I felt about myself. Not
evenings in the wood-paneled living room before the
roaring fireplace or the handfuls of good works that I
gathered daily and presented to God. The islanders' warm
words, their gifts, were for minister's wife, not for me. But
minister's wife, that display model me, was cracking. At
last, I cried to God for wholeness.

Within months, my world seemed to come to an end.
Jack's doctor warned him that he was a coronary candidate
and agreed that he would be wise to resign from the
pastorate.

We packed full-time Christian service in trunks and

boxes and stored it with our furniture in an empty basement. Where would we go? We were 3000 miles from family and friends. Outside of the people in the communities in which we'd served, we knew almost no one in the West. Had the God who'd parented us in New York City—the God who'd continued to father us for nearly eleven years in the Northwest, suddenly become preoccupied with the Milky Way? Had his attention been diverted by some fading star? God, we knew, was not a bumbling Divinity; he was perfect Parent.

A family we'd met when we first arrived in the Northwest allowed us to rest for an extended time in their off-the-road beach house in another part of the state. As Jack rested, his health began to improve.

The house offered me a vacationer's identity. Ahead, I assured myself, would be another ministry. God would allow me to find significance in Christian service in another town, in another role. Meanwhile, I prepared can-opener meals and served them on paper plates. We sat at the oilcloth-covered table in front of the picture window after meals and watched for secrets in the water. Afternoons, we walked the beach and filled our pockets with shells and our minds with prayers. These were parenthetical times when we studied starfish and tasted the preciousness of single moments.

Jack took a trip to look for a house for us to rent. We'd prayed that God would lead him to the right state, the right town, and the right house, and when he returned and told us that he'd rented a house in a small city in a neighboring state, we accepted it as God's will.

For several days we slept on the floor of our new home before the furniture arrived, covering up the last tenant's traces with beige, blue, and green paint. I made cheese sandwiches on a cardboard box for lunch; we brought in hamburgers for dinner; our sons explored the radio dial for new stations while we ate. When our furniture did arrive, we filled the rooms with beds with familiar lumps and hung our framed motto: "Christ is the head of this home, the unseen guest at every meal, the silent listener to every conversation."

This house wasn't a parsonage; church friends didn't make their way to the back door with a loaf of home-baked bread or a casserole to fill our stomachs and warm our arrival. We were only the new family on the block who had three boys and a white Chevrolet. Neighbors told us which supermarkets offered the best sales, where the laundromat was, when city buses left for town, and how our boys could find summer work picking strawberries and beans. Red roses had begun their summer climb up the white trellis in the front yard.

I felt my way around in my new surroundings, trying to touch the sides of my life. Early evenings when we took a drive, I caught glimpses of families behind curtained windows where they sat at evening meals, bursting with the day's activities. Townspeople in their own cars stopped beside us at red lights. They hummed along with their radios or drummed their fingers on the steering wheel, and when the light turned green, they drove to their own houses, opened their own doors, and walked into their own darkened living rooms.

Jack was able to work; we remodeled a room in our home as the center for an audiovisual ministry—a work in which Jack was experienced. With our savings, we bought equipment and supported ourselves while we began film production, but before many months passed, we'd nearly run out of money. Jack had to find a job.

Without full-time Christian service to depend upon for status, I squeezed my wife and motherhood roles of every drop of identity they could provide. My "see what I've been doing" projects began after breakfast and lasted until nighttime prayers. I refinished an $8.00 desk, made a rug from thrift shop woolen scraps, drapes from dimestore muslin, curtains and pillow covers from recycled bedspreads.

I scooped up every Sunday opportunity to do lay Christian work, and added a Wednesday night Bible class and a weekday home Bible study, but lay Christian was an ego-stabbing facsimile of full-time Christian worker, and wife and mother were long-worn-out roles. For the first time in my adult life, I had no way to provide the sense of personhood I craved.

Jack hadn't turned up a single job lead. The seat in his only pair of suit pants had a gaping, unmendable hole. Our $1.00 thrift shop toaster no longer toasted, our electric frying pan no longer fried, and our electric iron no longer ironed. A corner of the living room housed our television sets—both of them, a portable atop a console. One set provided shadowy gray images, the other, sound.

During those days of zero bank balance, when entertainment was feeding peanuts to park squirrels, when life was reduced to finding enough money for the rent and for gas for the car, fear lodged itself like a fist in my chest and tears were a blink away. Expansive, top-of-the-crisis faith narrowed to a slit of hope. *Where was God?*

I begged for a quick, cliché solution, for God to provide a George Mueller, bread-for-the-orphans answer. Another Elijah and the ravens in the wilderness miracle—a five-minutes-to-zero-hour phone call offer of a job for Jack beginning tomorrow, a Holy Spirit motivated letter and check signed by a New York friend. I prayed that some wealthy contributor would breathe life into our dead audiovisual ministry. But phone calls were from telephone salesmen asking if I "had a minute to hear about a grand offer." Letters were usually marked "occupant."

Afternoons, when Jack was out looking for work and John Lee, Paul, and Mark were in school—when the mailman had come and gone—I sat on the couch and wept. *God cared about us only when we were inner circle, gospel-carrying professional Christians. When we were the Reverend and Mrs., we had status. Now that we're just pew believers, he's moved on to some other parsonage*

*couple. God doesn't care about me now that I'm just the
lady down the block—a frumpish, middle-aged housewife
whose importance in the world ends at her own front door.*

Life was a big, fat nothing.

Heavy with depression, I thought of ways to commit
suicide. A last-second decision to step in front of a
speeding car, and the misery of trying to live would be
over. But, although I didn't want to live, I didn't really
want to die, either. So I sat on the sofa and wept,
mourning for the Father who'd deserted me and for full-
time Christian service that lay moldering in a trunk.

One Sunday afternoon, after a morning standing and
sitting and swallowing tears in church, and a noon meal
thick with tension, I washed the dishes and, unable to
maintain a calm mother facade any longer, took my sorrow
out the door and down a main thoroughfare. Lawns were
scrubby grass. Gutters were littered with flattened paper
cups. Used car lots and gas stations were fast pushing
family residences to other streets. *It's as ugly as my own
life.*

I walked past people who were living their own
weekend lives. We were side-by-side strangers spending
our years polishing our cars and painting our fences, each
of us in isolation from the rest. Cars revved and zoomed
past me, going somewhere; I resented the men in suits
and ties and women in tailored pantsuits whose lives were
in working order.

I sobbed aloud at the men and women who drove
through Sunday, at the ones sitting behind their drapes
reading the newspapers, at my silent God. I walked, then
ran, sobbing louder: "God, where are you? Why, God?
Why?"

The next moment, the Lord of the day spoke without
a voice, yet as clearly as though someone had stepped out
into the doorway of the house I was passing: "Will you
trust me even though you don't understand what I am
doing? Decide right now."

The next moment, I found the answer exploding within. "Though he slay me, yet will I trust him."

In front of a Mr. and Mrs. house that was squeezed between a shabby rental with sheets covering the windows and a used car lot, I repeated the words. They pulsed through me, and with a thrust of will I offered them to God as my own vow: *Though he slay me, yet will I trust him.*

Job's words, spoken naked on an ash heap, were mine.

On the corner of the next block I walked into a burger and fries stand and, on a red plastic-covered bench, solemnized my declaration of faith without sight over a paper cupful of coffee. God was God, and that was enough.

Thirteen/ LOVED

A Sunday-only friend in the church we'd been attending
turned in her pew to exchange after-church handshakes.
"Have you been to the Women's Bible Study?" she
asked. "It's an interdenominational group that they call
the Friday Fellowship. Marge is such a great teacher. I
can't tell you what she's meant to me."

She pointed to a brief announcement in the bulletin,
one sandwiched between choir rehearsal and a summary of
the year's giving to date. "Friday Fellowship meets at 9:30
A.M. in the church basement."

The following Friday, I locked last of the week routine
behind the front door to be put on with my apron when I
returned and walked around the corner and down the
street past the stubby lawns, used car lots, and the
restaurant where I'd solemnized my vow to God.

I imagined Mark bent over his desk on the second
floor of the school as I passed it. I peered through parted
kitchen curtains in houses along the streets for glimpses of
women washing dishes or baking cakes. On the other side
of the railroad tracks, the empty brick synagogue waited
for sundown when West Coast Jews, cousins of those in
New York City who'd sold us hard rolls and cream cheese

in family delicatessens, would put on yarmulkes and hold the Star-of-David-embellished synagogue door open for their wives. I imagined them inside, treading softly on the centuries.

Except for an occasional elderly woman pulling a shopping cart or a young woman pulling a toddler by the hand, the sidewalk blocks were empty. They were mine. During these moments, there was no one to peer into my soul or to speculate on my state of contentment. I could move unnoticed in my sidewalk world with strangers held at bay behind their doors and windows and speculate on their happiness. I could even cultivate safe, imagination friendships. In my mind, I saw women inside the houses and apartments turn and smile at me. I saw them open their windows for a chat and their doors to invite me inside.

Around the corner, past a gas station and a laundry, to the church on the corner. I hesitated at the idea of leaving the city sidewalk-boundary to enter the church where I might have to manufacture "I'm fine's" to match "How are ya's," when what I yearned to do was to rip off my Christian facade and reveal ugly soul sores.

But I turned and followed the sidewalk path into the brick church, down the stairs and into the large basement room that had been decorated orange and black at halloween and red and green at Christmas. This morning, casually-dressed young women and matrons wearing afternoon dresses with pearls at the neck stood in knots of chatter, edged with fences of private laughter. The few women I knew were already drawn into their own private friendship circles. I slipped to the coffee urn, drew a cup, and, clinging to the wall, edged as inconspicuously as I could to a rear seat.

I put my purse on the floor in the square inches allotted me, arranged my Bible and notebook on my lap, and folded into myself. *Why isn't this my class to teach? Why is this other woman waiting for the moment to stand in front? Why not me? Why have I been shelved?*

"It's time, ladies," Marilyn, one of those from my
own church announced from the front of the room.
Women spilled laughter on each other as they filled the
seats; right-and-left-chair women laughed "excuse me's"
as they tried to settle beside me in their own square inches
of space. Low last remarks to neighbors, husky side-by-side
whispers, and they settled around me, finally making me a
part of themselves.

Marilyn's welcome-mat remarks, her verbal
handshakes, were like cries of delight because her favorite
cousin from Tuscaloosa had unexpectedly come to visit.
After one more special reminder and one more group
song, Marge stood and faced us.

She studied our faces as though beginning a separate
conversation with each of us. Finally, she spoke:

"I love you. I want you to know that."

She stood silent for moments, loving us with her eyes,
and then spoke again, emphasizing each word.

"I love you, and God loves you, too."

I stared at her. *Love me? How can you love me? I'm a
stranger—a nobody. You don't even know me. How can
you possibly love me?*

I wanted to believe her words, to press them to me as
though they were an embrace from God. Could they be
true? *Does this woman really love me? Does God really
love me?*

"It's true, Marion. Believe her. She does love you,
and I do love you, too," God the Holy Spirit confirmed to
my inner self.

True. Once and for all. Forever and ever, amen. God
loves Marion Siegel of the welfare Siegels, daughter of
insanity, called Jew. He loves her intimately.

Marge spoke God-words for an hour. "I love you with
God's kind of love," she told my teenaged self. "It
doesn't matter what you're like. I don't have to get to
know you before I decide whether to love you or not. God

loves you exactly as you are, and he is loving you through me." It was as though God's love had suddenly been made visible and tangible.

Back toward home, past the gas station and laundry, past houses. Now, though, I didn't create imaginary friendships as I walked the blocks. Now I was content to let the women putter in their kitchens, mindless that I'd passed. Now, my child-self jumped up and down within, circling, squealing, and singing: *God loves me. God loves me.*

I felt the way I had when I became engaged to Jack in New York City. Then, love had been at my side. Love held my hand and anticipated my desires. Jack bought me a gardenia from a street vendor and pinned it to my coat. He sat beside me in Central Park and trusted me with his most secret dreams. Now I knew that love—more than human, from the beginning, perfect Father-love was mine.

Week after week, month after month, I locked the door behind me and went to the church basement to listen to Marge talk about God's unconditional love. I was like a child who kept climbing back up on her father's lap, settling down in his warmth, my head against his chest, and pleading: "Tell me again, Tell me again about how when I was born and you first saw me, you thought I was beautiful and you loved me so much."

Friday Fellowship women who'd experienced God's love themselves met me at the church door and stroked me with acceptance. They kept me from creeping to corners of the room and folding into myself. "I'm *so* glad you're here today," one would say and put her hand on my shoulder. "Have you had any of these delicious cookies?" another would ask and guide me to the refreshment table and into the group of women who'd gathered there.

A doctor's wife wrapped me in her friendship. Over coffee, she frankly revealed a less-than-perfect self. She didn't roleplay, but showed herself to be a person who was a wife and mother and who, in spite of doctor's-wife

prestige, succeeded and failed and needed God's help.
Together, we gathered around grace.

During the years before Friday Fellowship, when I'd
read Scriptures like, "See what a wealth of love the Father
has lavished on us, that we should be called the children
of God" (1 John 3:1), I'd tried to create a mental image
of God smiling at me and accepting me. I'd tried to feel a
God-Marion love reminiscent of the mother-child love I'd
sensed during springtime walks in the woods, but my
dwarfed self-image refused to allow me to really believe
that God could love me in Father-child fashion. Although
I knew Jesus Christ as my Savior, I couldn't bring myself
to accept his love.

Love is a reward, my stunted self had insisted. *Love is
bestowed upon those who are acceptable—those who
achieve. Read the fine print in people's glances when they
are with you. Listen to their offhanded comments. Man
doesn't accept you. How could God really accept you?*

Now I saw God's love, incarnate in Marge and the
others at Friday Fellowship. I felt it in their words. I
experienced it as I rode in their cars and ate cake at their
kitchen tables.

God *loves* me! He loves *me!*

Unqualifiedly!

God didn't want me to be reduced to a "nothing";
he wanted me to learn to become humbly submissive to
his Father-wisdom. His love was a fragile, chiffon truth
that I fingered tenderly. Between Fridays, I tried it on, as
though it were a garment too good to be worn, and
examined myself, dipping and twirling. *Look at me! God
loves me.*

But rejection memories had replayed themselves for so
long in my private screening room that most of the time I
still behaved like the old Marion Siegel Duckworth—the
one who had to have the smartest babies, the whitest
diapers, the most polished Christian life, and the longest
list of full-time Christian worker feats. The person within,

shaped by years of self-hatred, still felt unworthy. She flatly refused to let God's newly found love change her way of life. Knowledge that God loved me—that I could therefore love myself, seemed to be locked in a mental front parlor. Slavishly, I lived the old life.

One afternoon, not long after God had first whispered his love and I'd seen it incarnate in Friday Fellowship Christians, I was deep in normal routine, juggling housewife and mother projects in my kitchen and taking bows before God after each act.

At the kitchen counter, I spooned cookie dough in pans. A scorch-or-stir something for dinner simmered on a back burner of the stove. I eyed the clock: a dryerful of wash-and-wear clothes had to be removed in minutes. While I spooned, stirred, and clock-watched, I searched out of the window for Mark and his friend from down the block who were playing run, dive, and flop in the backyard, and tried to concentrate on the Bible lesson that a radio minister was teaching. Ecclesiasticism in the kitchen, like mottoes on the walls and a Bible in the hand, meant nods from God.

Commands shoved against one another in my mind. "Scrub the sink with cleanser. What kind of housekeeper are you? Smooth out every wrinkle in the bedspread. There's a spot on the counter. Get it off. *Now.* Move . . . *move!*"

Help, God, I prayed. *Speak in firecracker fashion so I can hear you over the clamor of Monday through Sunday. Save me from myself.*

But resident self-hatred held doggedly to its place as patriarch of my life.

Fourteen/ DISCIPLINED

We'd been living for about six months without a regular
income. During that time, Jack had worked in the harvest
on a mint farm for two weeks, then as a freelance
television news cameraman. I planned meals around the
"reduced for quick sale" shelves in the supermarket as
well as the beans and cornmeal that a neighbor gave me.
Hamburgers, the staff of life, had become treats. I'd
prayed for a Red Sea miracle; God hadn't provided one.
We needed some kind of miracle—fast.

I know that you know what you're doing, Lord, I
prayed. *But I don't know what you're doing. You're still
my God—even though I don't understand your
silence—but I'd feel better if you'd let me know what's
going on. Ever since I cried for help to discover who I am,
things have fallen apart. Why, Lord? What do you want
me to do? Look for a job myself? Would that be taking
matters into my own hands? Would I please you more if I
wait for a miracle or if I look for a job? You don't really
want me to go to work, do you? Not after a seventeen-year
layoff!*

I prayed and waited for a check to arrive in the mail
or at the door. I prayed and waited for the phone to ring.

I prayed and waited for a personnel manager to welcome Jack into his office, shake his hand enthusiastically, and say, "You're just the man we've been looking for!" But after praying and waiting for God to leap tall buildings with a single bound and facing only silence, I became more convinced that God did want me to look for a job.

But, Lord, any wife—even those who don't know you—could solve her problem that way. I expected something more spectacular than that!

The idea persisted, however. But what kind of job should I look for? I could organize and teach Bible clubs, teach women's Bible classes, handle youth groups, superintend Sunday school, but these weren't marketable secular skills.

Perhaps I could get an office job. I'd typed church bulletins and sermon notes for Jack while he was in the ministry. I sat at the kitchen table and practiced: "Now is the time for all good men to come to the aid of their party," while my sons timed me by the second hand on the kitchen wall clock. Then, praying to find a job and hoping not to, I went to the State Employment Office where first-day-of-school jitters made me type q's instead of a's and semicolons instead of p's, and I failed my speed test. "Practice some more," the barely twenty-year-old interviewer advised gently, "and come back and try again."

My office skills simply weren't marketable in their present condition, and I didn't have time or money for a refresher course. What other kind of work could I do?

I'd worked as a salesclerk while I was going to high school. Could that be where God wanted me, ringing up purchases on a cash register behind a counter? *I'll make myself available at personnel offices, God, but you provide a job in some special way so that I'll know that it's your will for me.*

Dressed in my looking-for-a-job suit, I rode the bus to town a few days later and walked in the front door of my

favorite department store. As I rode the escalator, I
suddenly remembered that, as I passed this store a few
weeks before, I thought: *If I have to work, this is where
I'd like to get a job.* A sign posted in the doorway to the
employment office at the top of the escalator, though,
read: "Applications accepted only on Tuesday." The day
was Friday.

The following Sunday in church, a woman I knew
only casually leaned over and whispered: "I saw you on
Friday in the department store where I work. Are you
looking for a job?"

I told her that I was.

"Last week, the personnel manager asked me if I
could recommend someone to fill a sales position. I'll
speak to her on Monday and tell her about you."

On Tuesday I was hired.

I could see footprints of a miracle in the circumstances
of the last weeks. Not a "water into wine," or "fishes and
loaves into food for 5000" kind of miracle, but a God-
selected sequence of events that had begun with the
steady, inner conviction that he wanted me to look for a
job and ended over W-2 forms in the personnel director's
office. An above-the-circumstances, center-stage miracle, in
which God produced a fairy tale solution to my problem,
wouldn't have required me to come out from behind our
living room drapes and step into the secular world. Part of
me understood and smiled at him.

But another part of me shrunk with fear.

The first morning, transformed from customer to
employee by the store's "How to Be a Salesclerk" Manuals
I'd read, and the name tag on my dress, I followed the
personnel manager's assistant to my checkstand in the
men's department. She turned and asked: "Ever worked a
register before?"

"Not since I was in high school."

"It's easy. Don't touch this row of keys. Each
department has a letter code." She rattled off a list of

departments and their letters. "Ring the correct
department number first. The price next. Punch up all the
items, total, and there you are. Eleanor is the girl who'll
break you in, but she's out sick this week. If you have any
questions, just ask someone . . . ." and she turned and
headed across the store to the up escalator.

I was alone in a world that began at denim jackets
and ended at sweatshirts—the lone clerk on a checkstand
island surrounded by aisles full of men's blue jeans, work
shirts, boot socks, bandana handkerchiefs, and long
underwear. Other clerks, preoccupied strangers overseeing
Hardware and Ladies' Lingerie, were isolated on their own
islands. They were separated from me by displays of
tennis racquets and bathrobes, and by their practiced,
behind-the-register movements.

My checkstand desk was piled with the miscellany of
merchandising: credit card forms, credit applications,
refund forms, inventory sheets, lay-away forms . . . . What
did the instruction books say about lay-aways? What had I
read about the procedure for accepting a customer's check?
How was I supposed to handle a credit purchase?

I'd fail. I'd make some stupid mistake, and my
supervisor would march over to my checkstand red-faced
and announce: "That's it. You're through." I was too
old. My mind was too confused. I didn't have enough self-
confidence. I couldn't remember anything I'd read in
those training books. The other clerks were strangers;
they'd laugh across their checkstands at me if I asked for
help.

I can't do it, Lord. As I rang up the first sale, my
hands shook so violently that I could hardly keep my
fingers on the keys. *I want to go home. I don't want to be
a salesclerk.*

Another part of me replied: *Remember your empty
bank account. Remember: God has specifically directed
you to this job. He is with you and will help you. Trust
him. And remember, somehow he is going to use it for
your good.*

As the hours passed, my hands shook less. Clerks in Men's Suits were polite when I asked them to help me fill out forms during the day, and close out cash for the night. As I walked out of the store's rear door and returned an assistant manager's "Good night" at closing time, I thought: *Lord, I actually made it. Thank you.*

When Eleanor returned to work the following week, she greeted me with a broad grin and spent the next few days introducing me to the differences in styles of long underwear and blue jeans. With a practiced eye, she caught my mistakes instantly, corrected them, and went on to laugh with me over our sore feet. Human beings make mistakes, her attitude intimated. Learn from them and go on.

As I rode the bus to work each morning, I examined God's miracle. Ordinary events, not divine thunderbolts, they were wonders nevertheless. *It takes more faith to believe that he is working through commonplace (and even distasteful!) things than exciting, supernatural situations. But I know that nine-to-five is the way he is going to make me a whole person.*

Salesclerk wasn't a status-producing role behind which I could hide my tottering sense of who I was. It was simply a paid-by-the-hour job to step into in the morning and out of at night. But I was a human being standing side by side with other human beings, and I was doing my job every bit as well as they were.

Salesclerking was providing me with an opportunity to achieve simple accomplishments, to help me build a sense of self-esteem, like the early morning ritual when I announced my department number to the paymaster and received my cash. There was the satisfaction of helping a customer who asked: "Do you have any lightweight bathrobes? My husband is going on a trip and I need something that will pack easily," and I could lead her to our stack of robes and help her find the one she wanted. There was the satisfaction of greeting strangers with a smile when, not long ago, I'd run from acquaintances. When I

put down the inventory sheet I was working on to wait on
a customer and went back to it again without losing count,
I felt pleased with myself. One of the lockers in the
"employees only" section was mine, one of the names on
the weekly schedule was mine, and one of the Friday
paychecks was mine, too. These things made me feel as
though I was acquiring human identity. And God was
making it possible.

Lunch time. I ascended the escalator to the second
floor and went through the Employees Only door to my
locker, where I picked up my brown bag lunch, purse, and
book and stepped into the lunchroom. Here I was,
stepping over the line from the impersonal "May I help
you" store world into a shoulder-to-shoulder contact with
other salesclerks. These times, I shed my new self-
confidence and trust in God's help at the door.

The employees' lunchroom offered no lunch. Coin-
operated machines served soda pop, peanut-butter-spread
crackers, chocolate bars, Lifesavers, and gum. Tables
offered coffee-stained magazines. A nearly empty, rear
wall bulletin board was pinned with a note: "Want a free
kitten? See Bill in Toys." At front tables, Boys' Wear and
Infants' departments sat elbow to elbow, unwrapping tuna
fish sandwiches and salting hard boiled eggs. At another
the janitor slept, his head resting on his arms. Two
department heads chewed and talked in low tones at still
another.

I hurried past Boys' Wear and Infants as though they
were street corner strangers and headed for an empty table
in the corner between the candy machine and the bulletin
board. There, I hid myself behind a library book and a
cheese sandwich.

Boys' Wear spoke to Complaint Department:
"How're you coming with your afghan?"

Complaint Department reached into a bag at her feet.
"About half done. I'm making it in three colors. See?
How do you like the combination?"

Girls' Wear peeled an orange. "Were you short of help this morning like we were?"

Infants' chortled. "Short! Are you kidding? I worked alone!"

At the next table, Display Department rose. They crumbled their brown bags, threw them in the garbage can, and put their pop bottles in the box on the floor. Slapping shoulders and scattering haw-haws, they made their way out the door. I bit into a cookie and turned a page.

During a few noon hours, when another clerk from Men's Wear shared the same lunch time, we sat together and laughed away diets and tomorrow's sale. Usually, though, I sat alone, isolated from the others by yesterday. To me, the halls behind Employees Only were high school corridors, the lunch room a high school cafeteria, the clerks and supervisors students and teachers.

In my imagination, I saw myself entering the lunchroom. "Hi, gals," I smiled all around a nearly full table. "Think I'll join you. How's it going?"

"You had to ask. Sit down and cheer us up." I saw us talking and laughing through our cold chicken. Then, one word led to another and I heard myself say, "Yes, I am a Christian. Jesus Christ lives in me . . . ." And I saw every head turned toward me, every eye on me . . . .

But in reality lunch hours were always the same. Me, talking briefly with the few people in my own department, or eating in a secluded sandwich and book world. Me, storing my noon hour self in my locker but carrying guilt with me as I rode the escalator back down to shirts and pants.

I was beginning to understand, though, that God loved me, hangups and all, and that he would continue to heal me. "Trust me," he seemed to be saying. Every morning, I collected my brown bag lunch and my purse and rode the city bus downtown toward healing.

Fifteen/ RE-CREATED (1)

I signed the time sheet and rode the down escalator to my
main floor checkstand through the back-to-school rush,
Christmas ring-it-and-bag-it weeks, and into January sale
tables (a lone pair of orange slacks size 31 x 34, a pair of
pink and green plaid socks, dirty white dress shirts, a
mustard-colored bathrobe, and purple ties—all greatly
reduced). By the time January inventory crews had
tabulated every spool of thread and every greeting card,
Jack had found work in a newly opened television station.
About the time Display was hanging cardboard bunnies
carrying baskets of colored Easter eggs in every
department, I was handing a letter of resignation to the
personnel director. Summer was a snow flurry away, and
ten-year-old Mark would need his mother at home more
than we needed a second salary, Jack and I decided.

That summer, we moved into another house in the
same city. While Jack worked at his new job, the boys and
I rolled latex on walls and scrubbed and waxed floors. We
moved in, and I sewed drapes from catalogue material and
invited the neighbors in to see. Some evenings, Mark
pitched for his Little League team and we sat on the grass
and cheered every strike he threw. Other evenings, we

hunted cool breezes with our neighbors, either in our yard or theirs.

Mornings, as I stood at the kitchen sink washing dishes and looking out the window, I watched the bus stop at the corner, pick up commuters, and take them to jobs in offices and stores in town.

I was a brown-bag-lunch and two-coffee-break commuter for eight hours a day, too. I wore good shoes and hose without runs, and complained about being underpaid and overworked. I waited in line at the bank on Friday to cash my paycheck. The world accepted me as one like themselves. Wonderfully, gloriously, I felt like an acceptable human being! Thank you, Lord.

By putting me behind a counter, God had given me the opportunity to discover that I was an adequate human creature—that I could step into the world and be accepted by it on its own terms. When he forced me to go to work, it was as though he'd taken my hand and led me gently into the water and let the waves ripple around my ankles. Every clerk-customer exchange: "What can I help you find today?" and every few words over a sweatshirt or pair of boxer shorts made me feel accepted as a human being. Because God loved me, because my position as his child gave me identity, I didn't have to pose as a statue saint. Salesclerk wasn't a Rev. Mrs. title to hide my humanity behind. What a relief to be only Marion Duckworth of the Friday paycheck and the sore feet!

Because I'd had to work, I enjoyed staying home. I could clean out a closet and take a coffee break, plant pansies in the yard, and take another. On Friday mornings, I could lock the door behind me and go to Marge's Friday Fellowship Bible study. Now I sat, not in an out of the way corner seat, but in the center.

Writing, the theme of all my "What I Want to Be When I Grow Up" compositions, began to fill my mornings. I sold my first article on the first submission. Other sales followed it. Article ideas began to come while I was mixing breakfast pancakes. They came while I was scrubbing the bathtub. I scrawled possible titles like "Is Sunday School a Spectator Sport?" on batter-smeared scraps of paper and tucked them under a flour canister. "After the article I'm working on is finished," I thought, "I'll try that one. And then maybe . . . ."

But after working for the television station for about two years, Jack found himself unemployed again. Prices had been rising steadily; we hadn't been able to save money. Recession was just beginning to make the nation shiver; jobs in our city were becoming scarce.

I sensed that God wanted me to look for a job again. This time, I put on my looking-for-a-job suit without hesitating and answered a newspaper advertisement for a salesclerk. *Lord,* I prayed as I had before, *if you want me to work in this store, then help me get this job.* Less than a week later, I picked up my uniform and filled out a W-2 form. Work began on Monday.

This time I felt at home behind a cash register. I knew how to function as a salesclerk: company smile at nine o'clock curtain time. Practiced "What can I help you find?" greetings. Salesclerk was like wearing a masquerade costume for an evening. Underneath, I could still be me.

The store, a gourmet food specialty shop, was a slice of Fifth Avenue. Streakless windows. Welcome mat spread mornings in front of the door. Tuesday customers' fingerprints Windexed along with the stripping of the cash drawer on Tuesday night. Counter scrubbed with Formula 409.

It was general-store sized, Madison Avenue rustic. A pot of free special blend tea was the "potbellied stove." Specially manufactured barrels, dummied with cardboard boxes, were piled high with sardines from Norway.

Lingonberries from Sweden, chutney from England, oatmeal from Scotland, lined the shelves in inch-perfect rows alongside domestic watermelon pickles in thick syrup

and miniature cobs of cocktail corn. Baskets of imported
candy, angled according to latest marketing techniques,
lined the front of the store, a year-round Christmas glitter
of red and silver cellophane. A Neiman-Marcus version of
the penny candy case: old-fashioned horehound, rock
candy, foot-long licorice, and salt-water taffy. Hard candy
with chewy centers, chocolate centers, tangy-tart centers,
and fruit centers.

Mainly, though, we sold cheese. Large-eyed swiss from
Switzerland, medium-eyed swiss from Denmark, no-eyed
swiss from Finland. Cheddar ranging from bland to
tongue-biting. Creamy Port-Salut, clover green Sap Sago,
Danish blue, English Cheshire. Cheese to melt, grate,
shred, spread, and slice. And to go with the cheese, sticks
of salami and summer sausage piled high.

But management hadn't hired me to be merely a
"May I help you?" ring-it-and-bag-it clerk as I'd been
before. Here, I had to *sell*. Clerks were paid hostesses
among the cheeses, paid to meet customers at the door
with a smile on our faces and food samples in our hands.
"Hi," I was paid to say to every customer who stepped
across the doorsill. "Have a taste of our sausage."

"Mmmm, delicious," customer would usually say and
keep walking down the aisle. I was paid to persevere. "Try
our swiss; we're offering it a special price today.
Delicious, isn't it?" If the customer kept walking, I was
paid to follow him down the aisle on my own side of the
counter. "Have a taste of our cheddar spread. It's a blend
of cheeses . . . ." Company policy demanded that I play
the part of aggressor, and our bank balance insisted that I
comply.

Offering the first sample was almost fun. It was a
shopper's surprise; it made me Mrs. Good Gal. But the
second, the third sample, and the sales pitch that was
supposed to accompany them was not fun. Why couldn't I
just be *salesclerk* again and help a customer find a blue
shirt, size 17, and ring it and bag it? Why did I have to

risk being rejected—put down by strangers? I played a mental game of "he loves me, he loves me not," with every customer who walked through the doorway.

Here's a customer. Offer him samples. Sell. You're obliged to do your job whether or not you like it.

"Hello, there. How are you today? Have a taste . . . ."

Follow him down the aisle. Offer him another sample. Tell him why he should buy your product.

Even though I knew the truth—that I was an acceptable human being because God said so—I now found myself unable to act on that truth. Fear of a curled lip, of failure heaped on failure, bound me to yesterday again. My old body of truth (you are not acceptable) returned; it became the one that told me who I was at every clerk-customer confrontation.

"Morning. Have a taste of our sausage . . . . ."

Watch out, it whispered. *This customer looks as though he's just waiting to put you down. Better not try to sell him anything.*

Believing old truth, I stood between sausage and salami and watched the customer walk down the aisle from swiss to blue cheese alone.

Again. "Good afternoon. Try a taste of our sausage . . . ."

Never mind this one. He'll just ignore you, anyway.

Company rules were plain. "Give a sample of cheese to every customer. No exceptions. Tell every customer why the product is what he needs." And as an extra incentive, we each had to record our weekly sales of key products on a wall chart.

Ego read rejection on the faces of unsmiling customers. Ego shivered and cringed. It cowered and hid among its memories. It begged to be allowed to run and hide among the cheeses, to pretend preoccupation. At 10:05 A.M., I obeyed ego and scrubbed fingerprints from the glass case while a customer came in and strolled the aisles alone. At 10:06 A.M., I was ashamed, and stepped over ego to greet the next customer as he walked through the doorway.

"Try our sausage . . ." and, "Let me give you a sample of our cheese spread. It's a delightful blend . . . ."

Finally, management spoke: "Sample every customer. No exceptions. I've been watching you, and you're not doing it."

Ego sagged beneath censure. *Every customer? No, not every customer . . . .*

I turned to the cutting board and began slicing a giant wheel of cheddar into wedges, stretched clear plastic wrap around each slab, and piled them in the case. *Why can't I turn the corner to tomorrow and find myself whole? How can I fight forty years of fear?*

I walked around to the front of the cheese case. *Why can't I just cut cheese, build displays, order supplies, sweep the floor, and get my paycheck?* I rearranged white and yellow cheeses, piling wheels and blocks atop one another.

God, why won't you sweep through me like a proper Deity, spilling holiness in your wake? Why can't I have a miraculous, front-page experience that will leave me unafraid? Why do I have to keep stumbling through the days?

A knife-blade of first-century Damascus Road light flashed through my mind.

"I love you. Remember? My love gives you identity You can reach out to others. Go ahead. I'm here to help."

Slowly, I understood.

Every clerk-customer encounter was a practice session. Dozens of times every day, five days every week, I had to risk rejection. It was as though I'd returned to high school corridors, not as a welfare kid with a Jewish father in the insane asylum, but as a child of God Almighty, Creator of heaven and earth, Amen. I was standing in the middle of childhood, I was pushing the baby carriage down New York streets. I was washing a parsonage kitchen floor—and I was a whole person. I didn't have to depend upon color coordinated sweaters and skirts and loafers with a penny under the flap, super-white diapers, or status as a grade-A full-time Christian worker to tell me whether I was acceptable or not.

I see, Lord. Here, behind this particular counter at this particular time in my life, in this controlled environment, I'm learning new behavior. I know who in the world I am! I am your child. And because I know that, I can learn to extend myself to others.

Every customer-clerk encounter was an opportunity to establish a brief personal relationship. A smile. Casual conversation. I look into his face, he into mine. He likes my cheese and buys some; he doesn't like it, frowns, and walks away. Each success, each failure, is only part of my job. It doesn't tell me who in the world I am. It doesn't change how I feel about myself. God has already told me who I am—his child!

"Have a sample of our cheddar blend. It's great for snacks . . . ."

"No, I don't care for any."

"How about you, ma'am? Try our cheddar spread."

A failure; a success. Frowns; smiles. *I can do it, Lord. You're right. I can do it.*

I'd been reasoning with God. I'd alibied, I'd offered him excuses and stood behind the counter picking the scars off yesterday. *Poor baby,* I crooned. *Poor, poor baby. You don't have to speak to that customer if you don't want to.* And to God: *Of course, you understand how it is.*

I'd been rationalizing with God.

I'd like to obey you, Lord, but you see I can't because . . . . Because I'm afraid. Because I'll be hurt again, and I can't stand being hurt one more time.

Reasoning with the Almighty. Here in the store, on rural fields . . . *I'd speak to that person, but . . . I'd visit*

in that house, but . . . I'd stop working non-stop,
but . . . .

Was that really what I'd been like? Arguing with the
One who sits on the throne at the top of the universe?

Here, amid the cheeses and cold cuts, the horehound
drops and peppermint sticks, I'd learn to stop
rationalizing, to admit my failures, to be honest with
myself and with God. I'd outgrown childhood clothes,
now I'd learn to outgrow childhood fears.

Childhood fears were as inappropriate as ankle socks.
Yesterday's set of facts ("We don't want you, Jew. You
wear funny clothes and buy groceries with welfare coupons
instead of money. We don't want you.") should have
been bundled and dropped in a New York City trash can
on top of candy wrappers and half-eaten hot dogs when I
knelt before Jesus Christ. But they'd been lodged deep in
brain crevices and blended innocently with other sets of
facts (two plus two equals four; the capital of Turkey is
Istanbul). They were tyrants that marshaled fear and kept
will captive. They interpreted every slight, every rebuff as
new evidence that they were, indeed, truth.

Forgive me, Lord. I know now that perfect love really
does cast out fear.

Sixteen/ RE-CREATED (2)

Here in Madison Avenue rustic, we salespeople weren't
separated by department store aisles and up and down
escalators. Before store opening, during noon hours, and
during coffee breaks (those ten-minute morning and
afternoon slices of freedom) we gathered in the back room
combination lunchroom workroom for coffee pot intimacy.
During these times, my lunch hours weren't corner table
isolation from Ladies' Sportswear and Yard Goods. Here, I
experienced kitchen table familiarity; shared snatches of
last night and glimpses around the corner at Friday.

We were tired feet and sensible shoes, tuna salad
sandwiches and potato chips. Our refrigerators needed
cleaning out. Our checkbooks didn't balance. We had sons
who worried us and husbands who snored.

"I never get caught up. You should see my house."

"Mine, too. My ironing basket looks like the Leaning
Tower of Pisa."

"This weekend, I'm really going to work."

"This weekend, we're having company. I'll be in the
kitchen from Friday night until Sunday night."

We were all created creatures; dirt and the breath of
God. Day after day as we sat around the table and eyed

the clock, I learned to think of myself as one of them.

At our cutting boards in the store, we cut and wrapped cheese and moved into one another's lives, talking between customers about the times when we were so broke that hamburger was a treat. One confided that she was afraid to be alone; another that she was afraid to go to the dentist. Gradually, I took bits and pieces of myself out of hiding and showed them around. No one gasped; no one stared in horror. They nodded understanding and showed me bits of themselves in return.

In the department store, management had been an absent authority upstairs behind a desk writing out orders and checking sales figures, who came downstairs to head departmental meetings, to arrange displays, and to survey the area like an unfriendly mother-in-law. Here, management was at the next cutting board. There, salespeople kept customers waited on, shelves stocked and neat, inventory up to date, and forms filled out. Here, blue cheese "is cut like this, so it won't crumble and wrapped this way so it will hold its shape." Sharp cheddar was "cut like this"; milder cheddar "like this." "Knives are always cleaned like this, boards like this."

At first, I made mistakes every day. "That's OK," management assured me. "You'll learn from your mistakes. No one's perfect, you know."

But months later, I was still making mistakes. "Your cheese is wrapped too loosely. Look at it; it's dried out."

"You're cutting that all wrong. That's not how I showed you."

Now that I'd been trained in store operations, every correction was a blow to my pride. Ego drooped, sniffled, yearned for home where it could pout and wage wars of silence when criticized. Ego longed to hide its tears behind a brave little smile when put down; it wanted to run back to its living room where it could demand to be patted and pampered. But God had put me behind a counter where there was no one who would listen to ego's demands to "handle with care."

One afternoon, while I was stacking boxes and wiping counters, my son John and his fiancée came into the store. "We're going on a picnic," he told me. "We want to buy some cold cuts and stuff. Do you have a place where we could make sandwiches?"

I took him into the store's back room where he spread out bread and laid slices of meat on it. As he worked, the store manager walked through the room, looked at what John was doing, but made no comment. After he and his fiancée left, the manager stood across the cash register from me and said through clenched teeth: "Don't ever let that happen again."

Another salesperson, a teenager who stood nearby, overheard. I was humiliated. I wanted to grab my purse and sweater and run out the door and down the street crying like a child. I wanted to throw myself down on the grass in the park and lie on my stomach for the rest of the day. I wanted to sob out my story to someone who would understand how I felt, who would put their arm around my shoulder and murmur, "Poor thing. Poor, poor thing." I'd been shamed—disgraced—and in front of someone young enough to be my own child!

But the next moment (before I grabbed my purse and sweater and ran for the door), I sensed another set of responses working within me—ones motivated by God within. *Stand here and take it. Your embarrassment will pass in a few moments.*

Within moments, my embarrassment *was* gone. I carried no grudge, lapsed into no angry silence, slammed no doors. Before, I would have gritted my teeth, steeled my jaw, painted a smile of acceptance on my face, and played martyr, but the incident would have reached into my core and convinced me one more time that I was worthless, for self-worth rode a seesaw manipulated by criticism and compliments.

That incident became a reference point for other corrections. Each time I did accept criticism, God used the situation to make this new kind of behavior more of an automatic response than it had been before. *I see, Lord. I'm learning how to be wrong without hating myself.* I smiled at the cheese and bowed my heart before God.

After I faced a habit that needed to be changed, God gave me as many opportunities as I needed to learn new behavior. No habit was easy to overcome, but God was with me behind the counter, prodding me to face each new discovery about myself.

Another morning; another wait in the cold on the corner for the bus. Another day in company-issued uniform and name tag. Another old habit, born of self-hatred, to unlearn.

One of the first instructions I received when I began my job was: "Remember, always lock the back door behind you. Anyone could wander in and steal from us."

That morning, I'd pushed a cartful of candy from the storeroom through the back door and into the store and began filling shelves. About an hour later, when I discovered that I'd left the back door open and went for the key to lock it, another salesperson saw me and asked: "Was the door left unlocked?"

As though I'd been reading lines from a script memorized along with "Thanatopsis" and the spelling of Mississippi, I said: "Yes. *Someone* left it open."

Someone? What do I mean, someone left the door open? Someone didn't do it. I did it.

I had a pronoun problem.

I felt as though I'd been caught lying to my mother. I went back into the store and began filling baskets of candy. *How long have I been afraid to admit when I'm wrong, Lord? How long?*

I poured red and white peppermints into a red basket and remembered other mistakes I'd been afraid to admit. *Last week, when we were getting ready to open the store, the manager pointed to yesterday's dirty towels still on the counter. "Oh, oh," I told her. "We forgot to put the dirty towels in the laundry last night." But "we" hadn't forgotten. It was my responsibility, not the other clerk's.*

And a couple of weeks ago when another salesperson went to ring up a sale and showed me the open cash drawer, I'd ask innocently, "Did someone leave the drawer open?" "Someone" hadn't left it open. I was the last one to use the register. I left it open.

Piles of misused pronouns hidden in mental closets lay before God. *I've been doing that, Lord? I'm sorry. I'm ashamed.*

My pronoun problem hadn't begun here in the store. It began when I started to hate who I was. That hatred made me want to hide my mistakes. It had been repeated like fork to mouth or breathe in breathe out, until it was a reflex action. Infested with self-hatred, sure that one wrong made me all wrong, I'd learned to hide behind anonymous words like "someone" and "we." I'd thrown my mistakes in the garbage and buried them beneath yesterday's newspaper as though they were evidence of criminal acts. *No one must find out that I don't understand how to parse a sentence, that I failed the test. No one must know that I burned the cake, ruined the dress. No one must know that I feel afraid (angry, depressed, resentful). No one must know . . . .* I'd secreted failure between the cracks of the days of my life and stepped out into every morning, a gleaming super-Christian.

How can I expose my flaws to a gaping world? How can I begin to admit my mistakes and my failures even to myself? To you, Lord? To others?

"I love you," God's presence reminded me. "You are my child. You don't have to build an identity. I have given you identity. Be human. Remember, I put you here behind a counter in a uniform and sensible shoes to teach you to live like my child. Trust me."

A few days later, just before closing time, the manager asked, "Who swept the floor? They forgot this aisle."

I'll pretend I didn't hear her and go quickly into the back room. But instead, I called across the store: "I did it. I swept the floor."

She laughed and called back, "I thought I was the only one who was getting forgetful."

The next time it was just a little easier. "Who cut this piece of cheese?" She pointed to a scrawny, crooked wedge of swiss in the case.

My stomach flipped. "I did it," I answered.

Another time: "Who wrote up this order? It doesn't have any pickup date on it."

"Oh, oh. That's mine," I answered. "I forgot."

I fouled up. Blew it. Messed up. Goofed. I did it. Me. See? I'm human. "I forgot to wash the knives (clean the slicer, inventory the shelf, fill the teapot)." I did it. It was my fault, and look, I can see now that these things aren't Judgment Day sins.

None of my mistakes were really serious ones, only everyday "oops" and "uh-ohs." Every deviation from perfection had seemed felonious to me before. Now that I saw them in perspective, I could begin to talk about them to God and to others without feeling like a failure. I was learning to stand toe to toe with the crippling emotions that had caused me to practice perfectionism, to roleplay, to refuse to accept human status before.

Sometimes decades-old fears captured my mind again and made my hand shake and my stomach quiver. Before, those fears would have controlled my behavior. I began to see that they didn't have to control me. When I stepped out on faith in who I was in Jesus Christ, I could behave God's way despite my initial reaction. When I chose not to believe in my identity in him, I failed.

During noon hours, God provided opportunities for me to practice living as the "new" Marion, too. They were

mini-adventures outside the disciplinary environment of
the store where rules and management were God's
enforcers.

Some days after I ate my sandwich, I hurried out to
buy socks or a birthday card. On warm crocus days, I
simply wandered down the block for a ten-minute tourist
walk. On days when I couldn't bite into another tuna
sandwich, I walked to a restaurant on the next block for
the soup of the day.

*Ahead, waiting for the light, is the woman who
served with me as room mother three years ago. I haven't
seen her since; she won't remember me. I'll just duck in
this store until she goes past.*

But God was my Father during lunch hours, too.
"Don't run away. Speak to her."

I can't, Lord. I just can't.

Father God was silent.

When I tightened my flabby will and drew the shades
on used-to-be, I could fall in step with the woman on the
curb.

"Hi. I haven't seen you in a long time. How are
you?" I could say.

"Oh, hi, there. Do you work around here
somewhere?"

For other people, a routine event that would melt
into nine-to-five and be forgotten. For me, Iwo Jima.

Not always did I draw the shades on used-to-be. Many
times, I did duck in doorways or cross the street. When I
did, Father God was silent.

Noon hours when I sat over a bowl of soup in the
restaurant I had chances to speak with other salesclerks
who hurried to work at the dress shop and shoe store at
nine. They sat three stools away down the counter, putting
catsup on their hamburgers. They didn't see me stirring
my soup, because they were busy walking around inside
their own lives—talking with the counter girl, reading
newspaper headlines, or staring at after-work plans. But I

saw them, for yesterday's Marion was a sentry, watching, crying, wanting to flee, wishing for New York City lunch counter anonymity.

It was much harder to manage a "how are ya?" in the school-room-sized restaurant than it was on the street corner. Here, other noon hour patrons could judge my words between swallows. On Thursday over chicken noodle, I succeeded. On Monday over pea, I failed. My failures were missed opportunities to become free of old neuroses, but they didn't mean that I was a failure. I'd simply believed feelings of fear instead of God and behaved accordingly. *I'm sorry, Father. Give me a next time.*

On other noon hours, I had to return ill-fitting or damaged merchandise to the store where I purchased it. Before, Jack had done that for me, but now that I worked downtown, I had to do it myself.

A leg fell off the reclining chair that my sons and I had bought Jack for Father's Day. After a single use, a suitcase wouldn't close and had to be returned. I shook and sweated; fear crawled like spiders inside me. *What if they sneer and accuse me of misusing the suitcase? What if they won't take the chair back? What if they laugh at me?*

"What are you going to do this noon?" another salesperson would ask over morning coffee.

"I bought this pair of shoes. The brown ones. You know the ones. They fell apart, and I have to take them back today."

A couple of weeks later: "Going shopping this noon?"

"Not exactly. I bought this pair of pantyhose, and one leg is twisted. It was put together wrong, I guess. I'll have to take it back."

Again. "What's in the bag, Marion? Don't tell me—you have to take something back again. What is it with you lately? Everything you buy falls apart. Don't do any shopping for me, will you?"

Was all the faulty merchandise an accident? I didn't think so. Another of God's "have to's."

After about three months of exchanges and refunds, my purchases stopped losing legs and soles. By that time, God's lunch hour lessons had accomplished their purpose.

Through all my noon hour experiences, he'd been exposing me to possible shoulder shrugs and blank stares—such five-second ego-stabbing rejections as had reinforced my sense of failure all my life. Pushed from behind my circumstances and encouraged from within by the Spirit of God, ego was losing its abnormal control.

Seventeen/ RE-CREATED (3)

At home, I shed my uniform and sensible shoes for slacks and slippers and my name tag for "Honey" and "Mom." But although I hung salesperson in the closet with my uniform, God within wouldn't let me hang nine-to-five Marion Duckworth away, too. Nine-to-five Marion Duckworth—that person who caught the bus at the corner, who sold cheese to every customer and risked rejection, who was learning to say "I" instead of "we" or "someone," and who was learning to accept everyday criticism without crumbling, wasn't to be an in-store phenomenon. She was to become twenty-four-hour-a-day, seven-day-a-week *me*.

I'd been an emotional first-grader who'd had to leave the security of home and family for a cheese store-schoolroom because there management wouldn't handle my poor self-image tenderly, careful not to inflict bruises or cause tears. A structured environment was just the kind of discipline that I needed to outgrow old behavior and allow myself to begin growing into the new, re-created person God wanted me to be.

As I changed, my personal relationships began to change, too. I was less afraid to reveal my real self. When a neighbor told me of an inner conflict with which she'd been struggling, I confided "I've had the same problem."

"You? I can't believe it, except that I know you wouldn't lie. But you've never seemed to have the kinds of spiritual ups and downs that I have."

"I sure do. It's just that I've done a good job of hiding them."

My relationship with Jack began to change, too.

Since that day in the minister's study when my husband had given me a new name and a new identity, I'd hidden behind his masculinity and used his tenderness as an ego-soothing lotion, splashing myself with it to cover my poor self-image. *Kiss my life and make it well. Don't criticize. Don't push me out from behind you into the world. Be my strength.* Jack's love was a protective arm around my childhood self.

But now I was free to grow into a more mature relationship with my husband—one that began in small ways. In order to do this, I still needed God's prodding.

When Jack walked through the kitchen and remarked, "You missed a spot there in front of the sink when you waxed the floor," and I involuntarily stiffened, ready to play the role of brave but wounded wife accepting criticism, I sensed a Holy Spirit nudge and lowered my defenses. "What spot? Where? Oh, now I see it. I did miss it, didn't I?" and back to the chocolate pudding cooking on the stove.

Dozens of ordinary situations were opportunities to practice behaving as an adult wife. When Jack asked: "What's for dinner?" I answered "Pancakes . . . ."

"Pancakes? That's breakfast."

Automatically, I stiffened. Then another God nudge.

"Well, it's breakfast for dinner. But cheer up. We have your favorite kind of sausages to go with the pancakes, and batter-fried apple rings, too."

When I sewed the sleeve of the blouse I was making in backwards, instead of hiding it in the drawer when I saw Jack coming in the driveway, I was free to leave it on the table, say "Look what I did!" and laugh as I began to rip.

When Jack asked, "Who left the garage door unlocked?" I was free to answer, "Uh oh, I did it. Sorry."

When he asked me to call the insurance company and ask them why we still hadn't received a copy of our new policy after two months, I could answer, "OK. I'll do it first thing in the morning," instead of trying to figure how I could get out of doing something so unpleasant.

Now, Jack's casual, "Ah-hah, cobwebs on the ceiling," and, "Look. Ring around the collar," didn't crush my self-image. The person that I was becoming had cut the apron strings to old ways of thinking, and to old identities. I wasn't Marion Siegel of the welfare Siegels or Jack's wife or Paul's mother or Pastor's wife or salesclerk. I was God's child, a created creature with strengths and weaknesses, abilities and limitations. I didn't have to cringe at every offhanded remark. Because I didn't have to be *right* to feel good about myself, I could admit that I left the garage door open and even apologize, and I could laugh with my family when I served burnt cake for dinner.

I didn't realize what a strain my emotional immaturity had placed on our marriage until one evening when Jack returned home from an extended business trip, exhausted. From his sagging shoulders and stunted smile, I could see that his trip hadn't been successful. As he walked into the bedroom and put down his suitcase, he didn't have a single "Praise the Lord" to his name. Still wearing his jacket, he fell across the bed and lay there silent and motionless with his eyes closed.

Gently, I removed his jacket and sat next to him, rubbing his back. My husband was facing one of the blank walls of his life. At that moment, he felt like a failure. He needed a wife who was emotionally whole enough to understand his feelings and to accept him, instead of a wife who slid into depression when he was blue, as I'd always done before.

Now, Spirit light shined in my mind. *My husband is*

a human being, too! I've insisted that he be
perfect—never angry or anxious because I've depended on
him for emotional wholeness. My alter ego! My surrogate
self! That's what he's had to be. I've wanted a super-
Christian husband. I haven't allowed him to be human
any more than I've allowed myself to be human.

I see, Lord.

I leaned over and kissed Jack's cheek; he turned over
and kissed my hand.

As I ran his bath and turned down the bedcovers, I
remembered a Sunday afternoon several years ago. I'd
been sitting in the summer sun on the front step of our
house. My eyes were red from crying.

Lord, how can I glorify you if I fall apart at every
raised eyebrow? Help me not to crumble—to take every
terse remark as a personal affront. Help me not to be so
completely controlled by my environment.

I knew now that God had begun answering that
prayer when he put me behind a counter. *Jack and I no*
longer share a single nervous system. I can respond to his
needs now without secretely condemning him for being
down, because God has been healing my emotional self.

Months later, I read Ruth Bell Graham's words: "If
you are married, don't expect your husband to be to you
what only Jesus Christ Himself can be. Allow your
husband the privilege of being just a man" (*Decision, May*
1974).

Jack, just a man; me, just a woman.

We were mates. He was the right shoe; I the left. We
shared scrambled eggs and the morning paper, a flat tire
on the freeway; yesterdays and tomorrows. We shared a
kind of humanity that has flaws. We were both trying to
let God change us. Meanwhile, God loved and accepted
both of us just as we were.

This Marion Duckworth—the one who stepped off the
bus at 6 P.M., dropped purse on the bed, exchanged
uniform for slacks, and name tag for "Honey" and
"Mom"—was a *person*. She wasn't just tripartite wife,

mother, and full-time Christian worker as she'd once been. She was a *person* who filled many roles but wasn't dependent upon these roles for identity. Because I could accept myself that way now, my relationship with Jack was more adult than it had ever been. And now, I was to find that my relationship with my sons would mature as well.

Because God nudged me one evening during one of my regular 6 P.M. supper scurries, I began to see my mother-self with Spirit light. I'd charged through the front door that evening, changed clothes and, within minutes, was in the kitchen shaping hamburger into patties. There were breakfast dishes still in the drain to be put away. Vegetables for a supper salad had to be washed and cut up; rice had to be cooked. The kitchen table would have to be cleared of schoolbooks and baseballs before I could set it for dinner. The clothes hamper was bulging; my plants were drooping from lack of water, the living room simply had to be vacuumed.

I ran to the bathroom to sort a load of clothes while I waited for the water to boil. Back in the kitchen, I grabbed the lid from the steaming kettle and remembered that I'd forgotten to buy catsup for the hamburgers.

God within nudged. ''Ask one of the boys to dry the breakfast dishes.''

I stood stop-action. *I can't, Lord.*

I stood at the kitchen counter and looked into the living room where my sons sat staring at a television rerun. *I'm afraid to ask them to help me.*

I was ashamed. I wept soul tears before the Holy Presence. God, however, didn't change his mind. He communicated his will into my mind plainly a second time. ''Ask one of them to dry dishes.''

Instead, I took the dish towel from the hook and began to dry them myself. *What's the matter with me?* I wiped plates and stacked them on the shelf. *Why am I afraid to ask my sons' help?* I crept through the evening disgraced before God and ashamed of myself.

For weeks, I paced back and forth in the memory of

that suppertime. Had I misunderstood? Had I only
thought God was nudging me that evening? Why had it
been so important for me to ask for help? My sons all had
regular chores: they cleaned their rooms, fed and walked
the dog, washed dishes, mowed the lawn. They weren't
rebellious, although they might argue as a matter of
teenage principle about doing chores. Usually, though,
they came through.

At some moment in my mental pacing, I knew the
answer. *I can't stand to hear them say "no" to me. If they
argue, "Aw, Mom, I'm right in the middle of a show,"
I'd suppose that they are rejecting me, instead of just
rejecting my request. My children's acceptance of me was
essential to my sense of well-being.* I'd worked overtime
for years to make sure that they liked me.

Habit was hard to change. Except for the memory of
that God nudge at suppertime, I would have continued to
rehearse martyr-mother. But as I continued to develop a
healthier sense of who I was, new mother attitudes came
more naturally.

"I need you to vacuum the living room," I told one
son as he passed through the kitchen.

"Why me? I have to do dishes tonight."

Before God's discipline, I'd have thought: *Doesn't he
know how tired I am? If he loved me, he'd want to help
me. He doesn't really love me.* I'd have insisted that he do
the job, but ego would have stepped back twenty-five
years and relived old rejections.

Now, I simply answered: "I need help. We all have
to pitch in to get the work done," and smiled to myself as
he went to get the vacuum, mumbling, "It's just not
fair."

That scene was repeated with variations during the
next months. "Come take out the garbage, weed the
garden, sweep the garage, bathe the dog, run to the
store . . . ."

"No" became easier to say to my sons, even when I

knew it would earn their disapproval. With God's help, I was able to respond to them in ways that were best for their development more often, instead of ways that would make them like me.

Now that my feelings weren't hurt as easily as they'd been, I found myself experiencing another emotion when one of my sons slapped me with an "Oh, yeah?" or a "What'll you do if I say no?"

I got mad!

At first, I was delighted with myself. Anger! Hot, human anger!

Soon, though, it stopped being funny. And the first time that my new temper flared in an exchange with a son and I was able to apologize, I knew that another phase of my identity crisis was ending.

I'd been rushing to skim the top off morning housework before I caught the bus to work. There was still time to run a load of clothes through the washer while I made the beds. Though I knew that Mark was in the bathroom getting ready for school, I plowed through the door to get the clothes hamper.

He whirled around in front of the sink angrily. "Can't you knock?" he demanded.

"Well, I'm *sorry*," I spit back. I dragged the hamper into the utility room, flung jeans into one pile, towels into another. *Who does he think he is? I work hard so he'll have clean clothes to wear before I run for the bus and stand on my feet for eight hours, and he has the nerve to stand there and . . . .*

I threw towels into the machine, dumped soap on top of them, and turned the switch. Words bounced off the sides of my mind as I bent down and began checking jeans pockets. *Look at that. A nickel. A gum wrapper. A paper clip. A comb. Can't they even empty their pockets before they throw their clothes into the hamper for me to wash? And every sock is inside out. That is the absolute limit.*

A still quiet spot in my spirit interrupted: "Mark was

right. He is not a little boy any longer. I had no right to
burst into the bathroom while he was in there."

Apologize? Humiliate myself before my own child?
Surely he'll lose respect for me.

I found Mark sitting in the kitchen thumbing through
a comic book. "I'm sorry," I told him. "It was wrong of
me to barge into the bathroom while you were in there."

He glanced up at me. "I'm hungry," he said.

Eighteen/ TRUTH

Who am I?

I am Marion Duckworth, child of my Father.

When I reached out in the universe for God, he took up residence in me. But even though I was living in the Divine Presence, still I was operating on old ideas of who I was.

Marion Siegel of the welfare Siegels
Insanity's daughter
Called Jew.

I sucked a self out of roles

Wife
Mother
Minister's wife.

Until the morning when I finally screamed: "God help me: I don't know who I am!"

Cloaked in the obscurity of circumstances, God answered. "My beloved daughter" and "My loved child." He whispered in soundless Spirit words as I punched a cash register and cut cheese. Under his tutoring, I learned to believe in his love and to begin to behave in new ways.

But there have been times when I've responded to those old negative feelings about myself again. I reverted to roleplaying; I crossed the street to avoid speaking with someone, and cowered inside myself, sixteen again. Then, God became a temple Diety before whom I had to prostrate myself and back away. During those times, I felt orphaned in eternity.

No matter how hard I squeezed my eyes shut and prayed, *feelings* of faith in God's love and care wouldn't come. At those times, I felt frightened and unloved, even though he'd assured me that I was loved. I pleaded with him to overwhelm me with his divinity. *Be Moses on the mountaintop. Thunder your commandments. Shout over my fear.*

I read the Bible and prayed that words would jump from its pages, spiritually italicized: *Marion Duckworth, this is for you.* On my knees, I begged that my heart would pound as I read a passage. I pleaded that Bible reading times would be Christian carnivals. *Be dimensional, Lord. Interrupt the order of breakfast to dinner. Be more than words on paper. Just until I feel better—please?*

Each time, as soon as the feelings began to subside, I could act on truth again: *I am God's child; he loves me.*

One of my son's tugs-of-war between faith and feelings has helped me understand my own.

He was afraid of the dark. At bedtime, he saw shadows that moved just outside his bedroom window. He heard strange, creaking sounds. His stomach hurt. He felt a hard lump in his chest.

We prayed together. I'd reassure him: "God is here with you. He loves you and will take care of you. And Mommy and Daddy are in the next room."

"Stay here," he'd plead after final tuck-in. "Please? Just a minute more?" When I refused, he climbed out of bed and followed me to the living room, where he sat on the floor in a corner with his head in his hands.

Fear, the color of night, obscured his daytime faith in "God who created the sun and the birds and me, too."

Night after night, we reviewed the facts. "God is with you, and we are with you." Night after night, he lay in bed and stared at the shadows on the wall. He cried. He pleaded. He followed me into the living room. Each time he left his bed, we took him back, tucked him in again, and assured him that he was safe.

We turned on a small light in his room. We stayed extra minutes by his bed, repeating the facts: "God loves you and we love you. He is here and so are we."

"Mommy, what's that noise?" he'd call.

"That's just the screen door banging. I'll go fasten it."

"What's that?" he'd ask again.

"That's just a dog howling in someone's yard."

Gradually, he began to believe that the shadow on the wall was only the form of the tree outside his window. Mommy and Daddy really were in the next room. They would take care of him. He began to understand, too, that although it was dark to him, God could see in the dark.

Feelings of fear began to subside. Truth became his experience, and he slept.

God the Holy Spirit had been my bedtime Parent. He'd tucked me behind a counter and reassured me that he loved me and that, because I was his child, I didn't need to search other people's faces to find out who I was.

But when my own fears lumped in my chest, when self-hatred cast nighttime shadows on the walls of my mind, I pleaded for a God I could see or hear—a Parent who would sit by my bed until I didn't *feel* afraid anymore. The written Word of God and my Father's quiet inner assurance that he loved me weren't enough during those times.

Like my son, I had to learn to look beyond feelings to truth. I had to learn to believe God's truth no matter how I felt about myself at that moment. I had to learn to believe God's truth and choose to obey it even when I imagined that other people were laughing at me.

When God's truth became my consistent experience, negative feelings would fade.

Finally, one afternoon, I became tired of my own tug-of-war between faith and feelings. I sat down at my desk and moved aside the painted rock paperweight, the pile of unsorted papers, and tightened my sagging will until it was a solid core to wind my soul around.

I began a conversation with myself:

Just exactly what do you believe about God?

"I believe what the Bible says about him."

Be specific. Sit there and write out what you believe about him in your own words. Then, when your world begins to shrink to a high school corridor again, you'll have this affirmation to hang your faith on.

I wasn't sure it would work, but I felt compelled to begin writing:

"Thousands of prayers ago, I concluded that the Bible is truth—that it is God's personal message to me. It reveals his nature and his intentions toward man."

I remembered yellowed letters tied together in a bundle and stored on a closet shelf. Some had been written to me by my mother when I was a child; others she'd written to relatives. All of them, even ones addressed to someone else, expressed her character and nature in every sentence. Through the letters, she "lived" for me again.

"I believe that Jesus Christ is God in flesh. When I knelt on my pride in New York City and called Jesus' name into a dark universe, he accepted me. It was just as the Bible says: 'Everyone who believes that Jesus is the Christ has been born of God . . .' (1 John 5:1).

"Although God is without human dimension, he can focus himself in a one-to-one relationship with a walk-on-the-earth person. Personal, intimate relationships with Jacks and Marions. He doesn't love mankind; he loves each man. He loves me. He is more capable of a personal relationship with men than another man could be. When

God created me, he gave me human identity; when Jesus Christ became my Savior, I became a daughter of the living God.

"I know that God loves me, not because I always feel loved, but because the Bible says so plainly in passages like 1 John 4:19: 'We love because He first loved us.'"

I went on to paraphrase some of the Scripture verses in which God promised to care for his loved ones' needs, and then wrote: "I believe in the Holy Spirit. He is God and lives within every believer in Jesus Christ."

I stopped writing and looked at the paper in front of me. *I really do believe that the Genesis Creator lives in me!* I sprang to my feet and paced the green rug, desk to sofa, and back to desk.

Though I'd been a Christian and claimed to believe that God lived within me, and though I'd sensed his inner guidance from time to time, still self-hatred had looked over its shoulder at the visitor's room in the mental hospital, then at her place in the welfare office, and had denied that Marion Siegel Duckworth could be indwelled by God. God is for thrones and for mansions, not for tenements and back alleys, self-hatred insisted, denying biblical truth. To her, the doctrine of God living within a believer in Jesus Christ—of intimacy with Deity—was a diamond in Tiffany's window, one to admire, to long for, but to pass by.

Since I couldn't really believe wholeheartedly that he was within, I insisted that God-Marion communication be a series of fanfare announcements. At crisis times, God had obliged. He'd thundered Job's words silently: "Though He slay me, yet will I trust Him." He'd spoken silent instructions and encouragement, not in audible words, but in strongly pronounced thoughts that even I, with the sounds of inferiority pounding in my ears, understood.

I knew now that God had given me a nonphysical kind of hearing—a kind of seventh sense called a "human spirit." I'd wanted to experience communication with him in my physical body; he wanted to communicate to me in Spirit fashion—in a quiet inner knowing. Now that my personality conflict had been resolved and I knew who I was, I could believe that he lived within—not because I was Park Avenue or Waldorf Towers, but because the Bible said that he did. Because I wasn't so torn with self-hatred, I was ready to let God communicate with me quietly, through the Bible—to let him breathe the words alive and spread them across my mind and spirit.

My statement of faith was finally finished. I read it through and then sat holding it in my hand. *Are you willing to accept these words as your own body of truth? Tomorrow? Next week? Next year?*

"I will."

I reduced it to a few premises and committed them to memory. When I felt myself responding to old ideas of who I was, I remembered and, before God and his angels, reavowed my statement of faith: "These truths I believe." Then while faith healed my soul, I *did* something: baked golden loaves of bread, visited a lonely friend, walked through autumn leaves, or thinned rows of young carrots.

By the time the bread was baked or the rows thinned and tiny new carrots scrubbed and boiled for supper, the past had lost its control. Truth conquered fear and became my experience.

From God, I discovered who I am. Until middle age, I felt around in the dark for clues that would tell me who I was. I searched the years for human identification as though it had been lost on my way to adulthood, trying on one identity, finding it deficient, reaching for another sturdier, more promising self. Hunting the corners of creation for my self, I found others, hunting for their selves. Only when I reached outside the creation did I find my lost identity.

I found myself hidden in the mind of God, begun as his idea. Formed in mystery in a womb. Pushed by the last contraction into history, confounded by the bittersweet taste of life, of joy mingled with pain. I'd wept loneliness among millions of others who'd wept in their own loneliness, for I had lived in God's world, yet separated from him.

But God had become an historic Man—Deity wrapped in humanity. He walked the centuries listening to the sounds of the lonely ones, waiting for one of them to call his Name.

When I found Jesus Christ, I found myself. But the tangled threads of false selves were still wound tightly around my soul—threads that only the God of constellations and amoebas could untangle. When I cried, "God help me." He began the process.

As self-acceptance grew, false guilt faded. No longer was I driven to scrub and polish guilt from my life as though the stains on my soul were reflected in the stains on the kitchen sink and the dust on the living room floor. I learned to pray creatively, expressing my real self to God instead of rehearsing mechanical "up and down the notebook" monologues. No longer do I need to bundle up packets of accomplishments to placate Ego and to pile as bribes at God's feet.

Who am I?

I am a child of God Almighty.

I am a wife, but Wife is not who I am. I mother, but Mother is not a self. I write, but Writer is not my identity.

Who am I?

I am a creature of my Creator, one who had fallen from the nest and has been restored to it—one whom God is recreating in the Eden image.

Today is made up of moments lived in the lap of God.

Tomorrow will be a moment multiplied.

Mark's bedtime confusion one evening a few years ago gave me a fresh look at "moment" living. His day had been a bad one. He'd lost his temper, been warned, lost his temper again, had to sit in a corner, lost his temper a third time, and was spanked and sent to his room. That night he climbed in bed and scrunched against the wall. I sat on the edge of the bed and hoped that the normal bedtime routine would assure him that, in spite of his behavior, I loved him as much as ever.

"Are you ready to pray?" I asked.

Without answering me, he began. "God, I'm sorry I was bad today. Help me not to be bad tomorrow."

"Mom," he asked in a tiny voice when he finished praying, "is a day the only time that there is?"

I knew what he meant. "No," I told him. "There are hours."

"Yes," he broke in, springing up on one elbow. "And there are minutes, too."

I kissed him and turned out the light.

Tomorrow, we will both live in moments.